TUMBLED

A Memoir of Perseverance, Personal Growth & Magical Transformation

REL Print Group, a Hezzie Mae Publication
Duluth, MN 55804

Editorial Design & Artwork: Nooordic Creative Studio
Photography: Jamie Fudally, www.fudallyphoto.com

ISBN: 979-8-218-14199-8

REL Print Group, a Hezzie Mae Publication

Tumbled

Heather N. Wilde is an indie publisher, writer, speaker, artist, and trauma survivor. She is the author of *Tumbled: A Memoir or Perseverance, Personal Growth & Magical Transformation*, *Pig Tales and Popcorn: Patricia's Memoir*, and *Sell Your Book, Not Your Soul*. She watercolor-illustrated *Precious Child*, a timeless children's book. In 2023, Heather founded Hezzie Mae, an indie publishing company. She speaks on accountability, personal growth, and recovering from trauma with the potential to lead an extraordinary life.

This book is a true account of the recollections and experiences of my life. I want to stress that this is my story and my story alone - no corroboration was done with the people who danced their way into this book because it isn't their story. Also, the names and identifying characteristics of some people mentioned in this book have been changed to protect their privacy.

Content Warning: This book contains subject matter pertaining to emotional and sexual abuse.

Hezzie Mae
BOOK PUBLISHING

Duluth Minnesota

TUMBLED

A Memoir of Perseverance,
Personal Growth & Magical
Transformation

———————

HEATHER N.WILDE

www.HezzieMae.com

Dedication

For my three daughters.

Independent Warrior Daughter, may you always lean into a life that brings you peace and joy. You walk this planet to lead with strength, yet always remember to soften into the divine young lady you are.

Musical Passion Spark Daughter, may your sprite-like playfulness become your Northern Star and leave behind the trail of tears and stresses. You are here to be a light and to remind others to hum their tune without reservation.

Fierce Little Angel. Oh, my little love. You needed a reference to help you understand the journey you have been a part of with glorious ignorance. You entered this life to be my Spirit Guide, and I watch you offer blessings to everyone that shares your sacred space.

XOXO Momma Bear

"There is no greater agony than
bearing an untold story inside you."

– Maya Angelo,
Why the Caged Bird Sings

Prologue

I once had a run-in with royalty.

During my Minnesota teaching years, I wove myself into the hearty, traditional fabric of the teachers' union. As their influence diminished across the country, I took pride in representing my colleagues and the profession. Our neighboring state of Wisconsin had just removed the power of organized unions with Act 10 under the leadership of Scott Walker in 2015. Minnesota was passionate yet panicked to hold onto the unity and strength as long as possible. Often it felt like we were the underdog, as a career and bargaining unit, yearning for validation.

I tended to have a louder spirit and personality at union meetings. I came to provide laughs and lightheartedness, sometimes my voice taking center stage. I felt a leader needed to stand out with a presence; I wondered how much of this was the honest Heather and how much was an act. Regardless, I went so far as to wear fancy Kentucky Derby-style hats primarily for entertainment purposes.

A fellow educator and I were standing in the hallway at a union training session, joined by many teachers from the area. Gloria liked my hats, and she was pretty eccentric herself. We had been friends from a neighboring school district for a handful of years; we both taught high school English, and we always laughed through some of the intensity that came up during our union meetings.

Out of the blue, she asked me, "Do you believe in life after death?"

Say what? When had our friendship catapulted into that realm of conversation? I awkwardly stumbled through a vague answer. I implied I was "open to possibilities" as a non-answer.

She smiled and added, "I believe in a previous life you held great power. . .like a countess. I can see it."

Nobody had ever spoken to me about anything resembling a past life or a countess. What was she saying? While my mind reeled to process, my body spoke a different language. It responded without prompting.

"Ah…look at your reaction. That tells your truth."

I was still speechless, and my tears ran wild. I was mildly embarrassed, very perplexed, and seriously uncomfortable.

Our conversation ended just as quickly as it had started, and she shared her morsel of truth, "In a former life, I was the Princess and the Pea from the fairy tale."

I had lived a sheltered, stuffed-in-a-box life. Her admission about being THE Princess and the Pea gave me an easy out. Metaphorically, Gloria had lost me, and I could walk away convinced she was nuts. That way, I didn't have to analyze my thoughts and ridiculous tears.

I poked fun at Gloria and this story a handful of times in the upcoming years, with it always drawing a resounding laugh from my audience. There was comfort in being a part of the norm and sharing a chuckle over such a ridiculous story, yet deep down, I felt like I was betraying someone who had offered me a gift.

A Narrated Childhood

"Creative entitlement simply means believing that you are
allowed to be here and that - merely by being here - you
are allowed to have a voice and a vision of your own."

— Elizabeth Gilbert, *Big Magic: Creative Living Beyond Fear*

I'm here to tell you a story about a small-town, curly-haired girl who landed on this planet and floundered for a while before eventually finding her place. Her childhood doesn't hold any sensational stories, but there's just something about her adult journey that's a little different than many other humans walking the planet. It goes beyond her crazy hair and tattoos. You can be your own judge as you digest her story. However, I will say she is pretty freaking brave to pen and publish some of this stuff. As for me, I am just her lowly childhood narrator, trying to make a buck, buy some new shoes, and shed some light on the early parts of her story before she tells you the rest of it.

Heather's childhood looks like Norman Rockwell and Mary Englebright shacked up in the backwoods of Minnesota and had a baby. As a child of the 70s and 80s, she appeared to be cared for, fed, and provided with the societal necessities of life, including those stylish colored corduroy pants sets and Kangaroo tennis shoes. She grew up lower-middle class and had experience with food stamps and powdered milk, but she didn't know any better. Now as an adult, she still has a strong aversion to kidney bean goulash. Yuck!

Around the same time her younger sister, Ann, came into the world, economic hardship hit the country with the 1980 recession. Her dad was a real Grizzly Adams-type, so when he got laid off from the mine, he worked hard to pay their mortgage and bills. He sold his canoe, trapped beavers for their pelts, tied fish eggs for the local bait store, and cultivated wild rice from our northern waters with her uncle. What an outdoorsman! Little Heather sat beside him in their musty basement and got her fingers right into the bowl of salted fish eggs, scooping them into a tiny mesh cloth before tying it closed with bright-colored yarn. How much money do you think they got paid for selling fish eggs? It's not like it was caviar.

Once Heather's Mother got a full-time job at the local county building, finances got a little easier. But, oh, Mother was a tough cookie! That 5'2" German woman had a presence, although I wouldn't say it was as a natural-born leader. Shirley hated working a full-time job and dragged her feet every single day. Her boss's name was Rose, and Mother was never short of grievances after a day at work. Rose had high expectations that must have pressured Mother, so she made her boss sound like a born-again witch. I hate to laugh, but when Heather was around ten, Rose called to talk to Mother.

Heather bounced up to answer the phone, turned, and announced, "Mom, that old hag, Rose, is on the phone for you."

Do you think Heather learned those manners in Sunday School class? Boy, did Mother send out the stink eye before grabbing the phone out of Heather's hand. That poor little girl was announcing that her allegiances were with Mother, but Heather got a lecture about manners and phone etiquette. The real lesson coming her way was that she shouldn't repeat the negativities spoken within the walls of her home. Unfortunately, that was a rule she had to stick to often in the upcoming years.

When most little kids were running around on the playground or throwing rocks, not our little Heather. That girl was boy-crazy coming out of the womb, I swear! It's almost like she wanted a boy to ride up on a white horse and carry her off into the sunset. Sadly, she yearned for love and nurturing as early as kindergarten. Her heart was already craving something more at age six. I think she had a crush on a boy named Jason. Or was it Scot? You have to feel bad for that little peanut. Children should feel carefree and full of wonder, not worried about finding a boy to fill the gaps in their hearts.

I must admit that there were many "shoulds" in Heather's childhood. Mother had a lot of expectations and rules that took priority. She learned how to be conscientious about her toys and organization, cleanliness around the house, budgeting and money, and the importance of practicing organized religion, to name a few. Mother embraced life with caution: cover a public toilet seat with paper every time, don't kiss on the lips, watch for changing weather patterns, and we obviously need to calculate menstrual cycles far in advance! Undoubtedly, Heather had life painted as one big, scary world waiting to turn against her. She had all sense of curiosity knocked straight out of her, and adventure was purely ludicrous.

Heather's extended family was a significant part of her life growing up, and why wouldn't they be when they could fill a small auditorium? She had both sets of grandparents, 14 aunt and uncle pairs, and around 45 first cousins (does it matter after 30?) within spitting distance, besides the ones that had moved away. Damn! That's a lot of grandkids!

The two families definitely had distinctive vibes, but Heather loved the different family events because there was usually good food and playtime with cousins. She and Ann stayed at Grandma and Grandpa's every summer for a week. Heather didn't even know how lucky they were all those evenings when Grandpa loaded them in the car for moose runs down the backroads of Isabella, Minnesota. No wonder she still considers the moose one of her spirit animals; they are so darn majestic!

As Heather's childhood years passed, Mother's needs and demands became more recognizable. Are you kidding me? They were hard to miss! Her dad and Mother always seemed to be discussing the messy family dynamics within range of her ears, and Heather couldn't understand why and how her dad's family could make Mother feel so horribly!

Heather dreaded the mood swings, but mostly when those looks of unhappiness appeared on Mother's face because of something she had (or hadn't) done. Little Heather learned to sense Mother's spirit at a young age by watching her body language or feeling the energy in the air. It became a habit for Heather to try to stay two steps ahead of any off-setting situation. Sadly, it was no secret that the actions of others played a huge impact on Mother's overall peace, and Heather knew she didn't want to be a part of the problem. Damn! No wonder Heather struggled with co-dependency most of her life; she grew up believing she was responsible for others' feelings and happiness. She'd even mirror Mother's energy because it was simply unavoidable. Heavy.

The minute Heather became good at sensing the emotions of others around her, deep compassion bubbled up inside of her. She became sensitive, even intuitive, to people and events around her, which created a lot of "noise" in her head. She's not paying me for my opinion, but I personally think that's how she got lost. She didn't have space to hear or worry about her own needs; she was so damn concerned with everyone else. She even tucked in her dolls and stuffed animals at night, ensuring each felt cared for and safe. She was a little nurturer; if only she could have directed some of that love inward! Then, only hours later in the night, she'd be rocked by nightmares. She'd be sitting in bed, frozen in fear, like she sensed beings swirling or some invisible pressure in the room. Poor little thing! She'd get so agitated trying to break free until she'd finally dart downstairs to her parents.

"Go back to sleep. It was only a dream," they said.

It sure seemed more traumatic than "just" being a dream to me!

..

Heather and her sister, Ann, had five years between them, but it sure seemed like a lot more. As only siblings, it is surprising that they weren't closer. Sure, they played board games and built forts in the woods, but there always seemed to be a rift between them that prevented a deeper bond. Heather definitely got annoyed with her little sister and often used a holier-than-thou voice on Ann, but I could see something was still missing between them.

When they were younger, they often prayed before bed. Another "should." But that stubborn little Heather resisted praying for her sister.

Reciting her prayer it often ended with, "God bless mom and dad and our dog and cat...(pregnant pause), and I suppose Ann."

Damn, Girl! Where's the love? What was so uncomfortable about loving on your little sister?

..

Finally, a special best-friend bond came Heather's way when a new Baptist preacher moved into town. His daughter got placed in her 4th-grade class and became fast buds. A whole new magical world of sleepovers, giggles, and independence opened up for her. Heather dove headfirst into church with her new Preacher's Kid (PK) BFF, Jodi, which suited her just fine. She rekindled the religious movement within her immediate family, and everyone started being more purposeful about attending this Baptist church.

Oh, I have to tell this Mother's Day story. Dang, this had to be a difficult day in their household because it made my skin prickle. This Mother's Day in 1987, they didn't greet Mother with breakfast, flowers, or jewelry. Not even a card was ready that morning as they ate the warm blueberry muffins (made by Mother) and cereal at the table. And then they knew - they had forgotten Mother's Day. Damn. It is safe to say that the breakfast was paused, although not too many words were spoken by anyone around the table. That's the thing: the more upset Mother was, the fewer words came out. Her body language said enough. Now, in Heather's defense, she wasn't even old enough to have a job yet. Ann wasn't old enough to even understand money. This year, their dad hadn't made it a priority for whatever reason, and it simply slipped everyone's mind...until it didn't.

Heather didn't just feel guilty for hurting Mother on this Mother's Day; she truly felt toxic shame that she had failed. There is a big difference in how we carry that level of pain in our heart, soul, and body and whether or not we can release it and forgive ourselves. Heather held onto this shame well into adulthood, and this event simply stripped another layer of her self-worth and a craving to do better and try harder to receive love.

It's easy to see how badly Heather needed an escape, so it is no surprise she started hiding her nose within the pages of books. You would often find her tucked into a corner or under covers with a flashlight, transporting herself into the magical worlds and relationships outside Two Harbors, MN. Heather spent her babysitting earnings on books and bookmarks. She feverishly digested The Bobbsey Twins, The Babysitters Club, Choose Your Own Adventures, and Little House on the Prairie before heading deeper waters with Go Ask Alice, Sweet Valley High, and the works of Judy Blume. Anywhere she went, she knew how to escape. I feel like applauding her right now!

..

Growing into her pre-teen and teen years had the typical struggles, and most of Heather's were about her body's imperfections and continued efforts to keep everyone happy. Mother purchased this hideous posture straightener in 8th grade that forced her shoulders back. The thing looked like a dingy, old lady's bra! That poor girl felt humiliated having to wear it and change in the gym locker rooms. I don't blame her, and I wouldn't have wanted to wear it, either! Heather acquired nervous habits, too, including chewing her cheeks and scratching her head habitually. The more Mother told her to smile prettier with those straight teeth, the harder it got to be natural. I think she was fairly self-conscious and had plenty of nerves. Who wouldn't? Mother makes ME nervous.

Now we come to the juicy stuff when Heather starts making some dandy real-world choices, like boyfriends, jobs, and college. Quite honestly, this is when the real roller coaster ride begins, so I can't blame her for being protective of the rest of her story. She took many left turns, set many dumpster fires, took one for the team, landed on her ass, climbed another mountain, and slayed a monstrous dragon - you get the picture. I commend this woman for being so vulnerable and transparent because she is about to share the pieces of her life, and not everyone is brave enough to do that. She has her reasons, and I am convinced that they are pure. So, I humbly bow out and pass the microphone over to her. I give you Ms. Heather Wilde.

Before 2000

"Trust that your wounds are exactly as the universe
planned. They were divinely placed in your life in the
perfect order so that you could show up for them with love
and remember the light within."

– Gabby Bernstein, *The Universe Has Your Back: Transform Fear To Faith*

..

I was the girl that always got caught when I broke any rules. Either I sucked at lying, or I had one overly uptight guardian angel always turning me in to "the authorities." I only skipped ONE HOUR of high school the entire four years - and I got caught. Mr. D was an advisor for the Science Team, and he wrote me a pass to leave the school grounds to practice my orienteering skills on the football field. I brought along one of my best friends, Sarah. Once we left the school, our plans changed, and we sidestepped to her boyfriend's house. We met a bunch of other high schoolers there who skipped the whole day, hanging out in some sort of alternative universe where school was not a priority. After we visited for around 30 minutes, Sarah and I left and started walking back to school.

Sarah was my adventurous friend and danced in a completely alien world, filled with boys and parties and a lot less worry about rules. Showing up at her boyfriend's house made me feel like an out-of-character badass, and I liked it. However, that rebel was quickly placed back in line within a few minutes when one of our teachers spotted us off campus.

Mr. N's gym class also walked back to school from the baseball fields and saw us.

They chanted, "Skippers! You're in trouble!"

Sarah and I had walked down one of the busiest roads in town, not thinking to hide, or maybe we just didn't care. Or perhaps I sucked at breaking the rules. The Dean of Students met us in the hallway when we arrived. I was treading in unfamiliar waters and essentially crapping my pants, while Sarah didn't seem ruffled at all. Mr. S brought us into his office and stated that we were in trouble and that he would call our parents. I had NEVER been in trouble, never had a phone call home, and completely forgot how to breathe. Mr. S dialed Sarah's number first and discussed our insubordination with her mom. When it came to my turn, I lied and told him my mom was on lunch break, which she wasn't, but I was too scared to face the music.

I was grounded, and my parents lost faith in me, while Sarah's parents didn't bat an eyelash. Our friends laughed at me and how my parents were being so rigid. Mr. D was disappointed in me, and he told me as much. That was a very impactful 30-minute detour Sarah and I took that afternoon.

Over and over, I heard, "Trust is the easiest thing to lose and the hardest thing to earn back."

No shit, Sherlock.

There was one other time I wasn't where I was supposed to be. I skipped church youth group to talk (literally) with a boy at our town's waterfront break wall. Mother said she "sensed" that I wasn't at church. She and dad drove into town to see for themselves and magically went by the two of us talking in that parking lot. I distinctly remember that she pinned it on her 6th solid sense, and I never doubted that. This woman knew things! She also confronted me when she thought I was having sex with my high school sweetheart (I was), and those events solidified the theory about her reading my mind. I was looking over my shoulder regularly, searching for her watchful stare. Add that to the deep-seated belief that my actions were responsible for her happiness, and I became a daughter that would either stay frozen and accommodating or rebel. I froze up like a Minnesota lake in January with over a foot of ice.

..

We were a very formal family that held "family meetings" when something wasn't smooth sailing within the household. Not meeting Mother's needs was a resounding theme at these meetings. (I cannot think of any other reason why we held family meetings.) We held these semi-formal events in the living room, with everyone seated and quietly waiting for mom to call the meeting to order. Each meeting sounded the same and could have had a permanent script:

"You (the collective) aren't supporting me enough."

"I work. Your dad promised me I'd never have to work, but here we are. So you need to put in more effort."

Clean. Help. Don't sleep in too late. Do more.

To better reach the family goal, we had a scheduled cleaning night during the week. The family polished our small, 900-square-foot house Thursday evenings before Friday and the weekend. With all hands on deck, you would think we'd clean it quickly. Mother had a lot of pride in ownership, so each week was dusting, polishing, vacuuming, cleaning, and washing. My least favorite chore was taking everything off the glass-top end tables, removing the glass, wiping the crumbs from the tiny ledge, spraying down the glass, and finally replacing it and the prior contents. I have taken a stand in my home never to own a glass top-end table.

During summer breaks, our family cleaning nights morphed into a chore list left for Ann and me while Mother was at work. Let's just say we had her arrival pinned to the minute, and it was amazing what one could accomplish in a flurry. If she got off work at 4 pm and it took 15 minutes to drive home, Ann and I might have started the list around 4:05. On many days, those floors couldn't have been dry by the time she returned home.

Over the years, I have volleyed back and forth with my sense of responsibility to have a spotless house. Everybody knows having younger (and sometimes older) children guarantees a certain level of organizational chaos. Fear drove my desire for a clean and well-organized home more than the overall state of affairs around me. If my parent's or grandparents' car pulled into the driveway, it was a mad dash to stash and straighten before they entered my space. But, as I have leaned into my needs, I am discovering a natural flow for my home. I don't need to make excuses or apologize when people visit because, "Hey, we live here, and cobwebs will become decoration around mid-October."

..

I found my high school sweetheart when I was a sophomore in high school. When I say, "I found him," I really mean that I established a connection with this senior boy by declaring he had the nicest armpit hair of any boy on the basketball team. He appreciated the compliment, and so began our four-year relationship. I have fond memories of our times together as a young and in-love couple. Our families got along well. His sister was in my class, and she became a good friend. Life was easy. We were in love and on a journey together through our high school and early college years. I believed my knight in shining armor had arrived, and the direct path to my happily-ever-after was crystal clear.

As for the rest of my high school experiences, they fell into place, regardless of my insecurities. I had a steady boyfriend, friends, weeknights filled with the pep band, and plenty of teen outings. I landed a "modeling" experience for a couple of years at the local mall, where high school girls learned beauty tips, did still-life modeling in store windows, and delivered the Mall Fashion Show. I enjoyed this unique experience and met some great girls from the surrounding high schools, but I always felt like a fraud that didn't belong. I wasn't as pretty or talented as those other girls! That same self-doubting monster showed up when I was voted Junior Class Homecoming Princess. The morning of the class vote, I confidently checked a big X next to my name for Princess. Oh, how I wanted that crown!

A friend turned around and asked, "Who did you vote for? I voted for Sally."

I felt embarrassment and shame when she glanced at my ballot. I felt like I should apologize. Did people vote for me because of pity? I knew I wasn't popular, so I couldn't understand how the votes slanted my way. Even with positive experiences, I didn't have the self-confidence to embrace the honors.

Around this time, I started earning money working part-time jobs at a local drug store and later Hardee's. I thoroughly enjoyed the serious uptick of cash in my purse, yet I felt a lot of resentment when the schedule didn't come out the way I wanted, or I had to sacrifice time with friends or for homework. I even had to work on Christmas Eve! Is that even legal? My entitled self felt comfortable holding grievances about the job expectations and working conditions, and I never felt satisfied. I didn't get fired from anywhere, but if it got uncomfortable, I usually bailed and found something else.

Even though my weight wasn't an issue during high school, I was still hyper-sensitive and constantly compared myself to the girls around me. What did they have that I didn't? I believed skinny meant worthy of love, so I was already worried I might put on extra pounds someday! During my senior year, a boy I had previously had a crush on told me I had a flat butt. I had never considered this at my 110-pound weight. I went home, turned around, and looked at my butt in the mirror. He was right! I had a crazy, flat ass! For almost 30 years, I have had a flat ass. It hasn't changed much, regardless of being fit or pregnant or slender or fat. It is what it is because it is me. That simple comment from a tall and handsome boy plays like an endless loop: I am not perfect regardless of my weight.

As I moved into young adulthood, I couldn't maintain 110 pounds. I wasn't aware of health and balance or any notion of what my healthy weight should be. When my weight catapulted into the 130s and 140s, I figured I must have done something wrong; I wasn't good enough anymore. It must have been all those Snickers Blizzards from Dairy Queen! I shouldn't have asked for extra candy on each one! The summer of 1993 started my never-ending quest to return to the perfect, slim body, still attaching the number on the scale to my value.

..

As the end of my high school career drew close, I didn't explore many options outside the box for a college or career path. In high school, I was good at numbers and accounting, so I chose a business major. That seemed logical. Our local selection of colleges was reasonably strong, and I didn't consider any college out of town for a fresh start. I primarily stayed for my boyfriend, but my desires for more for myself, in terms of a career, college experience, or adulthood, were fairly quiet. There wasn't a push from anyone to "be the best you can be" or to "listen to what makes you happy," so I enrolled in the University of Minnesota, Duluth.

Many of my friends and my boyfriend also chose UMD for their college experience. I had been watching UMD Bulldog hockey most of my life and was familiar with the campus, so I was pretty confident of my success. After years of following the rules and earning solid grades in high school without much effort, my world started spiraling within a few short months of attending this large college campus with so much less structure. The classes were enormous compared to high school, and college life gave me a lot of freedom. Economics and Finite Math weren't all that interesting (or easy), and I wasn't finding my usual success. As another faceless student, it became easy to skip classes in the big lecture halls. By the second quarter at UMD, my GPA was crap after earning a D in World Regional Geography, and the sense of doom and guilt took over. I didn't have much tenacity to figure out what to change or improve as a college student. I just knew I was on the wrong path.

Amid the college chaos, my boyfriend and I broke up. We had been together for over four years, and I didn't know a world without him. His family was my family. The promise ring on my finger had hinted at our destiny to marry, but when those promises fell apart, I felt like someone had just taken away my roadmap. His struggles and life led him down a different path, and I respected him for taking that road, but what was I supposed to do now? I felt disoriented and lost.

One of my part-time summer jobs had me working as an assistant in the local school district office. My tasks varied, doing clerical duties for various professionals. A wise, witty Sicilian woman became a coworker and friend, and I worked with her for several years. She led the entire district's food service department and carried many responsibilities. During summers, Jean and I sat in a back office and plugged inventory numbers into an ancient computer with its equally archaic software system. The work was mundane and monotonous, and we always ended up punch-drunk after a few hours. We said words incorrectly and fumbled over the most simplistic task. We survived off of squirrel moments and side conversations. Jean's strong, direct personality was a sharp contrast to any mother figure in my life, yet that didn't intimidate me. I always knew her opinions came with genuine love and support. There was never anything passive-aggressive about Jean; my walls came down, and a goofy side of Heather emerged.

As my college years trekked on, we were able to work together on random breaks. She was always interested in my life, even more so regarding my relationship status.

I can still hear her sighing, "Oh, boy...."

She never judged; she wanted me to be happy and never settle for less than I deserved.

Her mantra was, "It ain't all white picket fences, Rookie."

..

My early 20s were a challenging time for me. I didn't trust many of my decisions or take the time to listen to my feelings and emotions. When UMD got more complicated, I doubted my career path choice. I must be in the wrong program; that's why this isn't working out. I usually retreated or changed paths if a situation became uncomfortable, and this seemed no different. Without much consideration, I transferred from UMD to Duluth Technical College before the end of my first year, switching tracks toward a career as a Certified Occupational Therapy Assistant. The smaller atmosphere and content-specific classes were good for me, and it seemed this career path might be a better fit.

It wasn't until this young adult chapter that I started drinking. I didn't know how to do it. It reminded me of my first time on the dance floor at The Place in middle school. The music would be thumping, and strobe lights pulsing. Everyone around me knew what they were doing and made it look so easy!

I felt the spotlight on me, "How do you even do this?"

Dancing is about being in flow and letting your body respond to the beat. Unfortunately, my life wasn't carefree and flowy, so dancing and trying new things were very uncomfortable.

Just the same, I didn't know what to expect from drinking. After my religious training, I assumed I would fall dead from the poison or get struck by the lightning of God. Neither happened. My first experience with alcohol was shared with a college girlfriend and bottles of Zima, the trendy clear malt liquor of the early 1990s.

"Do Zomething different."

Later we switched to vodka and Kool-Aid. I wasn't sure what the drinking hype was about because neither the taste nor the experience seemed worthy. But, at least I had ripped off the bandage and was no longer a drinking virgin.

As my internship for a Certified Occupational Therapy Assistant (COTA) program drew nearer, I felt uncomfortable. Over a year and a half, I volunteered at various local establishments that would hire a COTA. Most job opportunities came as an Activity Director at a nursing home, where I'd help the residents stay mobile and flexible. Some special needs centers and school districts hired COTAs, but in limited numbers. I wanted to be in the school system, but that was such a minimal market that it appeared hopeless.

Again, doubts crept into my thoughts, "What did I like about this potential career, and was I on the right path?" With a short timeframe to graduation, I hit the emergency brake to jump ship. The fear of not finding a job was enough risk for me to leave the program without finishing and start something completely different. I took a not-so-big leap across the bridge to the University of Wisconsin, Superior. By this point, I felt like a college-jumping pro.

"Look, Mother. I still have my shit together! Don't worry! I will find my path."

I enrolled in a secondary education program to become an English teacher. My devotion to storytelling and books had started before I was even in double digits. Books had been holding and saving me for years! I previously considered being an English teacher and thought it would be cool, but I only allowed that thought to sit for a short time. I didn't believe I was worthy of such a noble career path. It also had not crossed my mind that jumping into three colleges with three majors in a short time wasn't normal. Seeing the absolute truth would have made me uncomfortable, so I kept busy enough to ignore all the confusion.

I took summer classes and stacked credit loads to compensate for my lost time. UWS was a good fit for me since it was midsize and relatively personal. If I pushed hard, I would be one year behind and could graduate in five years.

..

During my topsy-turvy 20s, I met a boy. Matthew was a handsome hometown boy with his goals focused on education. He had oodles of charisma and usually held the upper hand in conversations. His parents were both teachers, and I liked the stability and confidence they held. He did all the right things to make me his girlfriend. He made romantic cassette tapes with mood music and homemade spaghetti dinners and tried to woo my family. Matt was a worthy catch after healing the wounds of the breakup with my high school sweetheart. After a handful of months of fairly committed dating, I recognized his personality made me nervous. Maybe it was his confidence that edged on controlling. Maybe I could sense his dedication to our relationship and knew it was moving too fast. Maybe I felt at home when I was a ball of anxiety.

He liked to drawl, "Reeeeelaaaaax."

When he told me to relax, it usually accomplished the opposite and made me anxious. I believed I needed to break up with him, so Mother, Dad and Ann loaded into the car to leave home for the evening. When they came home, Matthew was still there. He simply wouldn't accept my attempt to end the relationship. I was so codependent I couldn't even honor my need to break up with the boy! Six months later, we had a formal dinner with both parents on Matt's & my year anniversary. He pulled me into a bedroom and played Garth Brooks' "The River" on his guitar. It was a little rushed, and he got frustrated when his mom walked in and interrupted. I sensed the elevated nerves and energy between the two of them. My gift was a box that could fit a small recliner, and inside was a bigger-than-life stuffed bear holding a heart sign asking me to marry him. Matt had his grandmother's diamond engagement ring, which he held out to me, on display for both families. A colossal life decision was in front of me, along with six sets of eyes awaiting my decision. I had a boy who loved me and wanted me as his wife. I accepted.

Since we weren't getting married for over 18 months, the wedding talk was always an open-ended conversation rather than concrete plans. We chatted about the bigger details like the date, church, and reception hall, but we didn't commit to anything. The upcoming months had a lot of moving pieces. My fiancé had finished up his first year as a teacher in a school about an hour away. He had developed some stomach issues that had him under the weather and concerned. He also took a job over the summer that kept him busy and out of town. At some point, he decided we shouldn't be intimate anymore, mainly for some sort of ethical, religious reasoning. I felt like distance grew between us, and my already nervous tendencies were not helping matters.

"Relax," was always his answer.

We decided to get married in a Lutheran Church for its capacity despite neither of us belonging to it; this didn't bode well on my home front. Matthew's family was Lutheran and still practicing, but our house was not.

Mother cornered me and accused me, "Why would you get married there? I didn't raise you to do this. I didn't take a stand for you to get married in a Lutheran church."

Lutherans were one of the"bad" habits she had removed from my dad when they married. Mother's side of the family was rich with Baptist ties (although most were the non-attending type), while my dad's side was still practicing Lutherans. We weren't even attending a church during this snapshot of my life. If anything, attending services with Matt and his family was the most church I had seen in a while. I didn't mind that the practices were different than what I was used to; the trade-off was going to church with my future family and feeling like I belonged.

I don't remember how this discussion ended with Mother. We didn't need to book anything yet, so I think it all fell to the wayside, and we ignored the uncomfortable conversation.

..

I spent the summer of 1996 with friends and living it up. Matthew was working in the backwoods with his logging friend and rarely around. I felt a growing rift between us but wasn't thinking much about it. I hated to admit I felt carefree and joyful, away from the weight of my serious fiancé. He was distant, and we were not together as much as we used to be. In my world, there were bonfires and parties to attend... many along the shores of Lake Superior. I had gained a certain comfort in drinking after my college stints, and I enjoyed living a life that was a little riskier. Consorting with a younger crowd at these parties became much more fun. At this point in my life, one side of the grass did seem to be greener and more enjoyable.

I thought I had my life mapped out. I was on my way to graduating from college and becoming a teacher. My fiancé was already on his teaching path. We were just one year out from our wedding. That space between us was so evident due to our busy schedules and different friend groups, but I was oblivious to how shaky our foundation was. I completely ignored the red flags and kept living my life. One particular boy at all of these parties kept capturing my attention, and his name was Leif. The temperature for the perfect storm had emerged as the man that loved me was not often in the picture. I had proven I wasn't stable enough to stay with one person, one college, or one career path. I was always looking to secure the instant gratification of what was "best."

It takes two to tango. While I was drawn into this web of friends and partying, Matt didn't want more time with me. The change in our relationship became a slippery slope, and I allowed my emotional state to take over. I felt utterly lost and torn between what I had and what I didn't.

I called off the wedding and relationship with Matt in a very immature, unplanned way. At the end of summer, I was at the point of no return: I knew I couldn't get married to him. Understandably, he also sensed something was off. At a girlfriend's wedding, we had a substantial public argument that resulted in his yelling and my throwing the engagement ring at him. Matt called me out on something irresponsible I had done, and that was all I needed to jump ship and pick a new course.

Before I was brave enough to close the chapter with Matt, there was the circumstance of a wedding dress. That summer, my mom and I went wedding dress shopping together. It was an impromptu opportunity that didn't carry a lot of pomp and circumstance. It didn't have a "Say Yes to the Dress" vibe. I wasn't very enthusiastic. My heart was a mess, and I wasn't strong enough to figure out the things I needed to figure out. I had dug myself into one big-ass hole. I tried on some dresses and found a rather beautiful one. Mother knew it was "the one" and wanted it ordered. I stood on a small riser in a pristine dress shop and looked in the many mirrors.

Mother insisted, "That's the one! We need to buy it!"

I stared at the reflection of a confused girl who felt like a fraud, but in my weakness, I simply caved and ordered the dress. Unfortunately, we called the wedding off before the nonrefundable dress arrived at the boutique.

..

The three-year age gap between Leif and me seemed more evident as the end of summer drew closer. The fling with him was a quick flash in the pan before he went off to his first year of college. I was, admittedly, madly in love with him, and it felt like losing a limb when he left. School life was his focus, and he enjoyed the freedom away from home. He partied hard, which caused some severe separation anxiety with me since we were apart. I lived for the weekends; he would drive home and hold me in his arms. It felt like I could finally take a full breath of air.

We woke up together one blissful Fall Saturday morning after having been apart for a couple of weeks. The phone rang, and his mother called to tell him his dad wanted to go grouse hunting that day. As I lay next to him, I felt a dagger pierce my heart. He didn't choose me, and I was devastated. Leif left shortly after the call, and I didn't spend time with him that weekend. I started to cling a little tighter, hoping to secure more time with him. We broke up a few months later when he called off our relationship.

I used the excuse, "It was just too painful for us to be apart."

There was a lot more at play, and most of that pain was coming from my side. What I wanted and what he wanted were two different things, and we parted ways.

..

I focused on my remaining college classes, working almost full-time at a local car dealership and preparing for 16 weeks of student teaching. Finally, in the Spring of 1998, my hard work and adjustments rewarded me with an English Education degree and a teaching job two hours away. A tiny farming community hired me for their K-12 school, teaching middle and high school English. This leap into adulthood was a busy, mind-numbing experience. The move across the state into a studio apartment felt like an extension of college life, but now I would earn a decent paycheck.

By this point, I had a new boyfriend that I had worked hard to commit to me over the course of the year. I played cat and mouse with Guy for a long time, which was hard to understand. I didn't know the rules of this game. I kept pushing and pulling, and finally, he agreed we could officially announce we were dating. After I moved out of town to teach, we tried to visit most weekends.

Guy was never a good fit for me. He liked stringing me along, offering friendship and intimacy with the hope for more. My bruised heart started feeling more desperate as the trail of former boyfriends was lengthening. By this point, I had received a promise ring from my high school sweetheart, a proposal from Matthew, and my heart supercharged from Leif. Guy was the next replacement. A relationship with Guy would not be the first time I'd force something that should be allowed to run its course.

..

When I landed that first teaching experience in a rural tourist town, my rose-colored glasses did not prepare me for the upcoming adventure. I wanted to come in and capture the attention and respect of all the students with my dynamic and creative lessons. I think the word you are searching for is "naive." Not only did the students resist my spelling lessons and sentence diagramming demonstrations, but college didn't prepare me to deal with mental health concerns, family loss, abuse, and addiction. I feel safe saying that many teachers went into the field with a warm, fuzzy vision of engaging young minds into loving novels and feeling well-versed in figurative language modalities.

In this town, most of the families were hard-working and blue-collar. Few residents had training beyond high school, which suited them just fine. I had been in college for five years, and I didn't expect the school and community climate to be much different from my experience as a high school student. Soon into the school year, I assigned detention to a squirrely 8th-grade boy who was disrupting every 7th hour of the day. My jaw needed to be picked up off the floor when his dad called to inform me his son would not be serving detention (ever) because he had football practice. The boy's dad told me that it was not open for discussion. My 24-year-old self earned a wounded ego and my first realization that teaching English would be more than opening books. A parent had already challenged my discipline style, and I slunk back behind my desk. I had lost round one, and that boy held his head high and remained unruly the rest of the term. So began the list of names I would never use for my children: LUKE.

On a positive note, I had the honor of teaching a young lady named Michelle. She was an 8th grader with a quiet and mature soul. Mere weeks before I became her teacher, her little brother tragically died at the county fair during a wagon accident. He would have been a 1st grader at our school. At college, we learned about lesson plans and the new state graduation standards, but the training didn't prepare us for the traumas that would enter our classroom (let alone a whole community). It was evident that the past 24 years of my sheltered life did no favors to prepare me for these situations, so I learned as I went. Michelle had such a gentle spirit; she held up her grieving family in many ways. Her inner beauty, tenacity, and grace earned my utmost respect.

That first year of teaching, I also came down with every illness, germ, and contagion that entered that school building, and I'd never been sicker. I had colds, bronchitis, pneumonia, and a horrendous intestinal flu that made me miss a meaningful funeral. I adopted a kitten that I named Vader to keep me company in the little studio apartment, and he was my buddy during my bout of bronchitis and pneumonia. That little black nugget and I shared this haven, and its coziness worked fine for us. I decorated with many Wizard of Oz souvenirs, ate a fair amount of Taco Tuesday deals and Muggs Pizza, and celebrated football Sundays with my new friends and coworkers. I was adulting.

..

I met another amazing human in Isle, MN, and I believe it changed the course of my life. Her name was Elizabeth, and she was a senior at Isle High School where I was teaching. I wasn't looking for a friend, or even deeper connection; I was focused on surviving my first year as a teacher. I didn't have Liz as a student in the classroom, but she was one of my yearbook editors that I got to know through our forced late-night deadline sessions. There were six years between us, but we were a great team, and the long hours were more fun than effort.

The teaching year and the published yearbook were a success. The students had learned while in my classroom. I was already formulating new, innovative ideas to implement for the next school year with full intentions of returning. We held a grand school party in the spring and unveiled our published yearbook. We invited our school board members to serve barbeque to the students while they sat on the lawn, lost in the pages of their yearbooks. The book was a success, and the administration was happy that the Yearbook Account was in the black.

"The superintendent is so thrilled with the yearbook! He said we could purchase a new camera for the Yearbook staff next year! Thank you so much for all of your hard work!" I beamed at Liz and hugged her.

..

I had accomplished some fantastic milestones graduating from college and completing a full year of teaching. I still dated Guy, and we had found a comfortable rhythm. My finances were healthy, and I even picked up a summer job at a golf course. Everything was as "it should be," yet I was still drifting. I wasn't happy. Memories and regrets from the past were holding on tightly, and my mind didn't ever stop thinking. I didn't know how to relax. I knew it was wrong, but I couldn't stop thinking about Leif. He haunted my sleep. I had never been good at processing emotions with certainty; I had so much self-doubt. Relationships were at the top of that list. I was frozen - unable to leave a boy I didn't love but unwilling to move toward what I wanted. I had worked so hard to convince Guy to love me: how could I be anything but happy? Leif had rejected me - more than once!

Then the actual dreams came, haunting me and leaving me restless and edgy. My thoughts started spiraling even more out of control. I had three specific dreams where Leif confessed his love for me, and we reunited, like in a rom-com. When I awoke, I was bubbling with anxiety and felt tortured.

"What would you do?" I asked a coworker, Jane. "I cannot stop thinking about Leif, but I have Guy back home. And these dreams! They are driving me nuts!"

"Oh, that is so romantic. I could never walk away from the signs your dreams are showing. But I think you need to consider your feelings toward Leif a little more seriously," Jane answered.

Her response just planted the seed of hope even deeper. With my brain and heart in overdrive, I asked a girlfriend back home how Leif was doing. It was horrible and beautiful at the same time. In my head,

I believed we were meant to be together and would reunite after our first spouses died. I wasn't even engaged to be married, but I already had my current partner with one foot in his grave.

As timing would have it, Guy was finally on board to get engaged. I had been pushing the subject for quite a few months, and he had resisted, saying he wasn't ready. Now that I was completely unsure about anything, I intuitively sensed he would propose soon. I should have been over the moon, but I wasn't. Word traveled back to Leif that an engagement was a near possibility in Heather's world - the gossip went both ways. Shortly after, a not-so-chance encounter ended with Leif and me in a hot tub with lots of truth and feelings coming out after some liquid courage.

As I stood next to my vehicle late in the night, making my exit, he stood next to me and said, "You belong with me. Give us another chance."

My life took an abrupt pivot, and I left Guy the next day without a backward glance. That poor young man never saw my split coming, and I am sure I gave him whiplash. I had been steering our relationship in one specific direction for a couple of years, and yet I was the one that ditched those plans with barely an explanation. That was the heartless part of me; believing my love for Leif made breaking another heart okay. Not only did I swiftly end and begin a new partnership, but I also resigned from my teaching position for the upcoming year to move back home. Those tender roots I had planted at my first teaching job were no contest to the galeforce winds pushing me into the arms of the man I had always wanted.

There was an audible exhale from my parents once Leif and I got engaged six months later; they had been holding their breath. At 24 years old, they had met many boyfriends, and the stakes kept getting higher as the years and break-ups ticked by, not to mention the numerous weddings of those before me. They wanted off this ride.

"Well, Heather finally ended up with the boy she wanted. Now she can be happy," my dad said.

I suppose they believed my husband would now be responsible for me - and they could wipe their hands clean and not worry about any "Heather relationship drama."

..

During the fall of 1999, Mother's mother passed away. Grandma S had been declining for several years and had moved from the farmstead to a small trailer, to my aunt's care, and finally to a nursing home close to my first teaching job in Isle. I didn't visit her much while she was there. My first year of teaching was hectic; I was sick often and didn't prioritize visiting her. If I have to be honest, I also didn't know how to. I didn't know how to face her as her mind and body withered away. At age 24, I had never attended a funeral, and I didn't understand how to face the natural process of declining life. Being such an emotional human, I was scared to become a blubbering mess. Trying to fight back the tears and emotions made me almost physically ill, and it was easier to fall into avoidance.

I moved back home temporarily for the summer after I left Isle (after Leif and I got back together) and happened to be there when the phone call came. Grandma was gone. Grandpa S had died many years ago, so the passing of Grandma made Mother an orphan, I suppose. As for me, I entered a foreign territory; I had never experienced death this close. I watched and sensed the actions I should take, much like a robot: go to bed, sit down, put an arm around Mother, and bow my head. As Mother cried, the magnitude of the situation became clearer, and I understood I would have to attend my first funeral.

I was so anxious about Grandma's funeral. What if I couldn't stop crying? What if I was the only one crying at all? Would my face turn all blotchy? Leif didn't take off work to attend, but I wished he had supported me. I remember standing in the outside vestibule with a handful of cousins. People were arriving and going in and out of the sanctuary. I had yet to sneak a peek inside. My Uncle Dick, Aunt Jenny, and three cousins gathered at the back and shed tears together as they walked in to say goodbye to Grandma. They comforted each other and held hands, and I saw a unique support system. It wasn't a picture I could imagine my family sharing.

Some cousins stood in the foyer with me, fidgeting, until it was time for the service to start. I felt sick. The heaviness in the air engulfed me during the speeches and numerous hymns, as I avoided looking at the open casket. Then, as we stood to leave, I glanced over once and saw the slightest profile of her face; she was pale and still. That was the most courage I could muster for my first funeral.

After the graveside service and family luncheon, I escaped to the car for the drive home. I decompressed and tried to bring my emotions back into check. I had survived and felt great relief, but there was no way I was going to stay at my parent's house that night. I needed to escape to the superficial world of a boyfriend, friends, and probably beer. As I exited the back porch of my parent's home, I sensed Mother entering the room before I saw her. She had had a long, emotional day and her face was tired. I assumed she was coming to tell me goodnight as I left, but that wasn't what happened.

Mother looked at me and said, "I am disappointed you were not there to support me more today."

I felt the weight of guilt and shame envelop my heart and body. I didn't know how to behave at a funeral. Nobody told me the rules. I hadn't done it right, and now I had let Mother down. I backed out of their house and felt defeated. What kind of daughter was I to disappoint Mother on one of the worst days of her life?

..

Somehow, my friendship with Liz had not disintegrated, and we stayed in regular contact as she moved off to college in the Cities, and I relocated back up the North Shore. The holiday season was upon us, and a group of friends had met at the Mall of America to shop, so Liz motored over from her dorm to join us. We were standing in the central amusement park area, alive with energy, when I asked her to be a bridesmaid in my upcoming wedding to Leif. Her response was immediate and sincere as if she had been waiting for me to ask.

Our mutual bond became open knowledge, and we leaned into a more profound friendship. Her energy was upbeat and goofy, and our souls sang together (actually, neither of us could carry a tune). She loved pickles and olives and popcorn. Her world and our friendship were playful yet meaningful. The age difference was irrelevant, and we were no longer teacher and student. This friendship felt different than any other I had experienced. Life became more carefree, so full of laughter. It was awakening just to have someone to share this level of friendship with. We would learn to trust each other with everything from boys and mother wounds to food cravings and teaching career dreams. She was my person.

Before 2012

"Let yourself be gutted. Let it open you. Start there."

— Cheryl Strayed, *Tiny Beautiful Things*

The ten months before our wedding weren't complete rainbows and unicorns, even though I chose to believe that. Leif was "my male person," and I was willing to take the good with the not-so-good. Drama inched into our relationship from the second we hooked up the previous summer. It seemed like rocky emotions, bickering, and unbalanced priorities were coming from both of us. We had been apart for over two years, and I think both of us believed we would morph back into who we used to be together. Instead, we had grown into different versions of ourselves, both with professional experience under our belt. Now we tried to plan for a wedding, build a house, and make adult decisions as a couple - it was a lot. When my feelings would get hurt, I tried to take control with anger, victimization, and silent treatments. If he could only see how he was making me feel, none of this would even be an issue! It took me many years to realize that I had no control over my husband (or any other human) and that I was responsible for myself.

We didn't have a long engagement, only five months. Everything started moving quickly once that ring was on my finger. When we couldn't find a reasonable home to purchase, his dad gifted us five acres off his forty. With his parents as our future neighbors, we started clearing and planning for a manufactured home to be brought in the following summer. It didn't occur to either of us the significant permanency we were putting into play, outside of our future marriage vows.

I was the last of seven friends to get married, so I had prepared for this moment for a long time. I was marrying Leif, and that was just the frosting on the cake! It was vitally important to me that my favorite area photographer, Keith Photography, documented our day. The wedding date was actually determined based on their availability. Our photographers didn't have a lot of last-minute options, so we settled on April 8th, one day after I turned 25 and only six days before Leif's 22nd birthday. So we would have one busy week in April to celebrate every year!

Wedding plans were easy and organized. I wasn't a high-maintenance bride. We attended a local church to find a pastor to marry us.

I had full intentions to raise my family as believers, so this felt logical. The pastor required marriage classes, implied that he wouldn't be used just for a wedding ceremony, and wanted confirmation that we would join his church. The reception venue was the ornate Moorish Room at the historic Greysolon Ballroom. Flowers, cake, bridesmaid dresses and shoes, and musical selections were all arranged. The only white elephant in the room (no pun intended) was that previously purchased wedding dress. I struggled to settle for that dress and felt like this was a new chapter. To wear the dress seemed like bad luck, regardless of whether I liked it. My parents reminded me of its cost and beauty. Both were practical explanations that took the emotions right out of the room. Why waste $600?

In desperation, I tried to alter the dress to look different. Unfortunately, alterations cost money and what I desired was a different dress. A seamstress removed some poof from the shoulders, but that didn't change anything. It looked almost the same, but I wore it. I had already given up my chance for my dream dress, so this was the price I'd pay. It didn't matter - all I wanted was the boy.

..

By this point, I had witnessed several bachelor parties, wedding eve parties, and receptions ending on less than a positive note. I was so worried that our experience would resemble any of those charades we had previously attended. Having control over those events and their outcome led me down a long, dark rabbit hole. I was paranoid about situations that would make me feel unimportant. Leif had already shown me that he differed from when we had been together three years ago. He was more stubborn and firm, not as affected by the rifts in our relationship. I didn't want there to be strippers at his bachelor party, and I didn't want him crazy drunk the night before our wedding or during the wedding reception. If I had thought he would sign a contract to relinquish his rights to these activities, I would have had it printed and notarized. I wanted my knight in armor to make this weekend about us - romantic and void of drama.

When he dropped me off after the rehearsal dinner, I made Leif promise to go right home.

"Could we please just get through the next 48 hours relatively sober?" I requested.

He promised he would head home and to bed, and I walked up the steps of the tiny rental cabin to spend my last night single with a best friend. We did the pre-wedding jitter chats and walked down memory lane, but I don't think I was present for her. Fear had taken over my thoughts and the possibility of Leif disappointing me.

Somewhere along the way, I had attached Leif's sobriety to his love for me. He must respect me if he didn't become a drunken ass at our wedding reception. How often had he shown me that I should be fearful of his choices with alcohol or respect? I never questioned if this anxiety might be troublesome or if he was the person I should marry. I didn't consider what it would feel like after the wedding reception. After the honeymoon. I never thought what everyday life would look like with Leif as my husband.

The wedding happened, and it was official - I was Heather Stevens. The man I had on a pedestal also had a ring on his finger, and we were a family. We left the church post haste and climbed into the back of a limo headed for the reception. The car pulled over a mile from the church as we poured a glass of champagne.

Our first conversation started as husband and wife, "I need to tell you something."

"Ok? Pour me a glass, please," I said, still in a state of adrenaline and wedded bliss.

"Everyone knows but you, so you should know."

Excuse me? My movement paused midair as I waited for him to speak again.

"I went out with Jack last night and didn't get home until 3 AM. My mom was so upset because we were drunk. I have been hungover all day and trying to keep it together."

"Everyone knows. Everyone knows but me."

My bridesmaids had been protecting me from the truth about my nauseous fiancé, now husband. My fears came alive. While I said my vows with tears streaming down my face, he was probably trying to keep from locking his knees and passing out. The little romantic love birds that circled over my head fell to the limo floor. Thus began our wedded bliss.

..

I truly loved this man. The way he smelled, his casual crooked smile, and his crazy curly hair. We made a great team. Clearing the land and building our new home was rewarding. This chapter felt so good, with both of us having good jobs that provided money to fulfill this dream. He continued being a welder with a steady income and benefits and worked a straight midnight rotation. I became a full-time educator at a local charter school that challenged my limited teaching abilities. Maintaining control was difficult for me (on so many levels), and this school had a student population that made my weaknesses apparent. I went home and cried almost daily. I believed feeling this way about a new career was adulthood, and I had seen plenty of adults that hated their jobs.

After watching a Sunday morning infomercial, Leif and I started exploring investing in real estate and rentals. We both had strong entrepreneurial sides, fueled by Leif's dream to retire in his mid-40s. I loved taking risks with him. Real estate conferences drew us from around the country, where we learned how to become landlords, flip houses, and dream big. We stepped out of the norm of friends and family, purchasing our first rental one year after we got married. I was 26, and he was only 23, and it felt like we had the world in the palm of our joined hands.

Those first seasons of our marriage were filled with fresh air, camping, hunting, and gardening. There were additions to our homestead with a beautiful deck and a larger-than-life garage. Step by step and piece by piece, we built our future. Early on, I wasn't aware it was in Leif's DNA to be a hobby farmer on our land. We had a huge vegetable garden and planted a variety of fruit trees. His mom gave him a birth-day book titled, *Raising Poultry the Modern Way.* I thought it was a gag gift, although I quickly discovered it was all serious. Chickens. We had never once talked about getting any feathered fowl, but low and behold, egg layers and meat birds came in rotation over the years.

While we established our homestead, questions like "when are we going to try to get pregnant" started to fire. Friends and family could see how much Leif loved babies, and there was never any question that he needed to be a dad. My idea was to have him to myself for a year, my needy side showing through, disguised as romance. The thrill of having babies with this man outweighed all the rest, and we started to try six months after we got married. Nature didn't take long to demon-strate its power, and we were pregnant and due the following summer. We were in the flow of life. It was almost like the Universe had set the boxes in front of us, and we just needed to keep checking them off.

..

Being pregnant the first time was hard; I will not lie. Being poked and prodded at medical appointments, as if spreading your legs in stir-rups was supposed to be a natural and comfortable . No room for mod-esty when you are growing a life! Hearing the baby's heartbeat for the first time made me cry. Seeing the swell start to show in the beginning was surreal. I had mild nausea that I could mostly manage. The first time I felt the flutter of butterfly kisses inside of me made up for all the uncomfortable growing pangs. The flutters turned into kicks that made my stomach morph like an alien trying to punch its way out. The intimacy of a baby growing inside of my body was barely describable. Hope and love grew for someone I hadn't even met, and there was nothing like it.

With this first pregnancy, there was one reasonably significant scare. I had a typical blood scan, and the results produced a positive screening.

At work, I received a phone call where the nurse at the other end offered this haste message: "Something came back with the bloodwork.

Therefore, I am scheduling you for genetic counseling and amniocentesis this afternoon."

I panicked. I raced home to meet my husband and get to the hospital. I wanted to throw up. I wanted answers. They lay me down on a metal table and administered the amniocentesis, inserting a needle that appeared a foot long into my belly. I was so scared that something was wrong genetically; I was just as scared that the needle would harm our baby. We went to the genetic counselor and discussed our families and their medical histories. When the results came back a few days later, they determined I had received a false positive the first time and that the baby was completely healthy.

We had glorious news to celebrate. However, the emotional toll of that week had left its mark as I broke out in a handful of shingles by my left side boob. It seemed unfair we had to endure all that for a false positive result, but other results would have been worse. I still have scars to remind me of the zap of trauma I felt that week in my hopes and prayers that our unborn child was healthy.

Pregnancy shed some extra light on my struggle with my identity and self-worth. My body was contorting and not looking so pretty anymore. I had retained a lot of water and could no longer wear shoes. I also had an older male doctor who suggested I might struggle to get all the weight off after giving birth if I didn't start watching what I ate.

"Lovely, and thank you for the advice."

Women don't discuss the potential feelings of loneliness and disconnection during pregnancy. I felt left out as I watched the lives of others go on as planned without any of the worries I had to carry. Since my husband regularly drank, I was the full-time designated driver. I was fueled by many mixed emotions every time I played the role.

"Can't we hang out at the gathering tonight? Maybe you don't drink, and we can watch people get stupid around us," I asked.

I could have been talking to a wall and received more support.

It was the perfect storm on a hotter-than-hell Saturday in July at eight months pregnant. Leif's sister was getting married, and the family had gathered for the formal pre-wedding pictures. I sat uncomfortably in a church pew with my whale-ish body, feeling anything but comfortable. I watched the photographer arrange family members for photos leading up to the traditional full family portrait. He posed the bride and groom, her parents, her two siblings, and her nephew. I had waited for someone to call me up to stand next to Leif as a valued member of this family. Pressure built up in my chest and worked its way up my throat; I stayed quiet when the invite didn't happen. Finally, when the emotions were ready to erupt, I rushed out and found myself in the church's creepy basement bathroom, where I released it all. I felt like an insignificant 8-month pregnant woman without a place.

..

One month later, we welcomed our daughter into the world on a glorious August day. After weeks of bloating and discomfort and a failed induction the previous week, she arrived when she was ready. She was proving to be a true Leo, boasting plenty of stubbornness, and required a C-section. Leif and I agreed to name her Michelle, after the beautiful young lady I had taught years before. During my post-surgery recovery, I shed 16 pounds of strictly water weight which seemed to impress the nurses. My body and mind were exhausted from hours of unsuccessful labor and a C-section. Michelle got a mild infection and developed a fever in her first days, making everyone nervous. Even with my need to gather all the peace I could, setting boundaries was not a part of my world yet. We swung open our hospital door and allowed 35-45 visitors in to celebrate her arrival. There wasn't a lot of rest and relaxation those few days.

While I drank the fancy hot tea cocktails to progress my first bowel movement, another side of me was distracted as I worried about my husband and if he was "happy." My mind told me I needed to keep him satisfied and remind him that I existed, even though I was the one recovering in the hospital bed. I wanted reassurance that we still had our intimate connection, even hours after having a baby.

"Please don't forget me and who we are," my eyes pleaded.

We brought our baby girl home, and Leif returned to work. He worked three 12-hour shifts (straight midnights) and then had three days off. At first, I was afraid to stay home alone at night with this newborn, even though I didn't have another option. I didn't trust myself NOT to mess up. The darkness of night seemed to make our hours home alone scarier. She was colicky, so I paced with the unhappy baby for hours and watched the hands on the clock slowly make their rotation. As the days turned to weeks, my confidence grew, and I found a rhythm with Michelle. My emotions swung in the other direction as I craved Leif's nights at work. My body and mind relaxed with no expectations but my own. At whatever hour we felt tired, I brought this little angel into bed and felt at peace with the world. We would sleep side by side deeply until the morning light. I had finally arrived.

Around the same time I had gotten pregnant, I also made a pivot with my job and left teaching. That particular school tested my classroom management skills tremendously, and I didn't want to end every workday in tears. However, I didn't leap entirely out of the educational world when I accepted an admission representative position at a local private two-year college. My role was still to encourage the value of education and specialized training; only now, it was from a sales lens. Admission and recruitment was my first higher-pressure sales experience, where my results were micro-managed by my boss and college owner, and it wasn't all that pleasant.

"Heather, did you see you have an unhappy face after your name in the board room? Too bad you didn't make numbers last week," a coworker said.

My workplace needed me to attend college fairs around the state when Michelle was three months old, and I grappled for balance. The worries multiplied tenfold as I now had to worry about a babysitter if Leif was working, whether or not I had enough milk pumped for Michelle, not to mention my mental and physical needs as a newer mother. On one of those college fair adventures, I found myself in a Herberger's parking lot, trying to pump discreetly in the front seat of my Chevy Lumina. It felt awkward and uncomfortable. Thirty minutes later, the camel's back broke when that pumped liquid gold spilled out onto my car floor mat. I felt guilty and thought a good mom would try harder, but my frazzled emotions needed calming, and "switching to formula was one step I could take to lighten my load.

My momma's intuition became more apparent, and our family found a rhythm. Having Michelle dependent on me gave me a new sense of purpose, and I clung to those warm feelings. Then, when she was nine months old, Leif and I discussed having a second child.

"I am close in age with my siblings, and I really like that," he said. "Wouldn't it be great for Michelle to have a brother or sister to play with a few years down the road?"

I couldn't help but compare his experience with mine, having five years separating me from my sister. It had hindered our ability to bond to some extent. The excitement of trying for another baby completely wrapped me up, and I didn't really pause and reflect if we were ready for the challenge. The Universe worked its magic, and Leif and I were expecting Baby #2 only two months later.

We had decided that I would stay home with our children and set aside my teaching career. It was a sacrifice, but I don't think I could have handled being a full-time mom and teacher simultaneously. So it made sense for me to work part-time around Leif's time off, still allowing some extra money to come into our account. Remembering my sacrifice the first time I got pregnant, I tried to make a deal with Leif for this second pregnancy. Funny, I might have still thought I had some "control" over his decisions. I told (not asked) him that he should also discontinue drinking for the nine months I was pregnant, especially since we now had the extra work of a toddler. That went over like a fart in church.

..

Thankfully, this pregnancy was much easier on my body. I savored having my last term over the colder Minnesota months compared to the sweltering heat of August while pregnant with Michelle. Even my body seemed to understand better how to handle pregnancy this time. I felt much more in control of my looks and weight, which went a long way in keeping my spirits up. I didn't retain 16 pounds of water, and my ankles didn't swell to the size of elephant feet. On the homefront, Michelle hit milestones and firsts while I grew a second child. We scheduled surgery for the next baby's delivery. I requested the delivery on 03-03-03, but my doctor didn't believe that an angel number birthdate was worth planning around. He made me wait until the next day (yes, the same doctor that told me I was fat).

As the days ticked closer to March 4, 2003, my emotions shifted from anticipation to terror. I looked at my 18-month-old daughter and wondered what I had done. This little one still needed my undivided attention. How could I even love another baby as much as Michelle or split my love in half? Would my heart stretch that much? Would I lose myself entirely - or my connection to my husband?

There was no compromise to be made with my fears, as a baby was still to be born. I walked into our labor and delivery ward and tucked my clothes and travel bag in the closet. I was hyper-aware of every poke, prod, and multiple attempts to insert the IV and catheter.

The nurse soothed my nerves and smartly remarked, "Relax. It's not that bad."

I call bullshit.

The nurse wheeled me into the surgical room with all the technical monitors, devices, and tools glaring under the bright lights. It looked pretty scary and different from the last time when I didn't have much awareness. Then I saw the eyes of my husband. He was masked with a face covering and a surgical hat, and I knew I wasn't alone. Together, we were about to welcome our second child into the world.

The anesthesiologist was one goofy, ginger dude, and I focused on his energy to guide me through the delivery.

Dr. G held up the baby and announced, "It is a girl!"

My response was, "You are lying."

For the birth of my two daughters, I wasn't allowed to wear glasses or contacts, so their tiny pink bodies were merely a blur. More than that, this pregnancy had been different, from the baby's heart rate, how my body carried the baby, and how I felt during the nine months. I firmly believed this baby was a boy, but Leif thought this second baby was a girl. We had a $40 wager on the table (quite literally). Unfortunately, our doctor was not in on the joke, and our 2nd daughter was born. We named her Leila.

..

So started life with two babies, two parents, one dog, and some chickens. It was hectic, exhausting, and numbing. Leif still worked midnight shifts, so I was on my own for 50% of the nights. Again, I felt like I was back at square one, learning to manage two children under the age of two. I didn't feel sane enough to consider doing anything outside of the home (besides church) until Leila was three or four months old.

Michelle accepted her new little sister with as much grace as her stubborn Leo side could. The only real hiccup we faced was for a couple of weeks when Leila was a few months old. The girls and I were at church planning for Vacation Bible School, and I tried to gather up my two littles to leave. With Baby Leila strapped to my chest and a diaper bag slung over my shoulder, Michelle decided to dip under and through all of the church pews. Gaining control over my two-year-old with a four-month-old strapped to my chest was like catching a greased pig. There wasn't much I could do besides keep my cool and wait for her to emerge. On the outside, I might have appeared calm, but inside, my lack of control created immense anxiety. I was more worried about how the drama looked to the church ladies who watched a defining moment with me as a mother. Our cat-and-mouse chase ended when Michelle decided this game could end, and we continued home.

Michelle was two years old the first time her dad drank and drove with her sitting in the car's front seat. I was somewhere with Leila, and Leif went to town with Michelle for smokes. He had consumed enough beer to think it was okay. I was hysterical.

"Are you freaking kidding me?" I yelled. "At what point did driving with Michelle out of her carseat - after you had already been drinking - seem like a good idea?"

Leif's drinking habits were a sensitive topic in our three-year-old marriage. I had learned that there was no amount that I could plead, threaten, or stomp in anger that could guilt him into drinking one less beverage or leaving the party when the time was appropriate.

For most of our marriage, I considered this a respect issue, not an alcohol issue. If Leif loved me or didn't like to hurt me, he would make a different decision. He'd choose a more respectable path if he wanted to be safe and set a good example around his daughters. We had created a relationship dynamic resembling a mother and son, where I needed to reprimand and guide him from his missteps. Looking back, I'm not sure Leif offered many apologies intending to change his patterned behaviors. Instead, I became the responsible one. I was the partner who drove us home from outings, holidays, and visits so Leif could drink. There were times when I joined in the partying, but I was constantly aware of the situation and knew when to slow down and sober up before I needed to drive us home.

..

Liz, my former yearbook editor and student, and her future husband Joe, had woven into our lives right from our wedding day. Leif and Joe didn't have a lot of choice in the matter since Liz and I declared our families were going to be close. The four of us were fantastic friends, spending weekends together fishing, camping, gaming, and exploring. That rhythm didn't change as our family grew, adding our two daughters. Michelle & Leila saw Liz and Joe as two of the safest people on the planet. Adoration exuded from Michelle whenever she was around Joe, and she could be found by his side, on his shoulders, or in his lap. That provided space for Liz & Leila's relationship to blossom, and their playful spirits danced well together.

The 2 ½ hour separation between our homes was never an issue. When we were all together, there were four adults for two children, and a certain synergy existed. We had a rhythm with everything - meals, evenings playing games, vacations. Admittedly, within that nucleus, there was a significant gender divide at play. The established roles were set: Liz & I were the responsible faith-driven organizers, while Leif & Joe were the more immature, rule-breaking followers. Liz and I both worked hard to control the outcomes of our activities, thinking we could keep these boys in line. Unfortunately, we took on that mothering role with them, which doesn't serve any relationship well.

One winter, the boys left before the sun to travel a few hours for a day of ice fishing. Their adventures would require scaling two different Minnesota mountains (large hills) with their gear to get to an inland lake. Liz and I started to get nervous when there was no word of their return drive as the day ended.

Anxieties grew, and a phone call was made to my dad, "At what point do we have to be worried enough to send search crews? Do you know exactly where they were fishing?"

My dad calmed my racing brain, and we continued to wait for them. The two of us sat on our hand-me-down couch with all the lights on, and we tried not to panic. The babes were tucked in bed, oblivious to the happenings outside their door. Liz and I waited and worried about the unknowns and possible tragedies, not to mention the area they visited lacked cell phone reception.

Finally, one of the two husbands answered their phone well into the night. Understanding they were both safe allowed us one exhaustive exhale. But, unfortunately, the tale that followed did not let us go to bed with any peace. Yes, they had made the early morning drive and suffered through a brutal winter hike into the wilderness. It had been more complicated than they had anticipated. But, presumably, they started their venture out with plenty of liquid warmth. After surmounting the first mountain, they found a snowmobile parked by another outdoor enthusiast. There was still one mountain left to tackle. I don't remember if they hot-wired it, but they made their trip back to the truck easier by stealing that person's sled. They didn't seem to feel guilty about the snowmobile theft because they had left an arrow in the snow, pointing the owner in the direction they could locate their sled.

These two knuckleheads drank the two-hour drive home, deciding to drive right past the turn to our house. Instead, they turned to the next road to a brother-in-law's garage. They had drunk the night away less than ten miles from where Liz and I sat worrying. When they finally returned home, there was much female squawking going on. I didn't learn, for a couple of years at least, to avoid any sort of discussion with drunk people. It was simply pointless. The following day, after a sleepless night, I felt second-hand shame and a healthy dose of anger as I stood in the shower. I cried tears of frustration as the water washed over me; this was not the first, nor last, appearance of tears in that private space.

"What if the person who owned the snowmobile needed it to get out safely, like an older person?"

"Why did they think this was so funny?"

My motherly yelling was behind our bedroom door before both couples joined the living room. The boys felt limited remorse and suggested we were overreacting.

After all, they said, "We left an arrow in the snow."

Leif sent numerous messages about his love and respect for me as his wife. He made these hurtful decisions regularly, but I clung to the belief that I could fix him, wake him, or make him treat me better. These experiences were simply a precursor of what was yet to come.

..

Mother's Day always came with so many expectations, and I carried those right into my own little family. Of course, I needed to honor Mother on this holiday, but I also craved my own recognition. Ever since the year we had missed Mother's Day when I was younger, it had become the grand-puba day with extremely high stakes. However, when I became a mother, I felt an imbalance. Where did her needs end and mine begin? I was in the messy middle, trying to find my place in the family hierarchy.

One Mother's Day, when the girls were little, I remember the need to set a new tone for the holiday. I wanted to spend the day up the shore of Lake Superior to hike and picnic with Leif and the girls. I decided to host a thoughtful event the day before, on Saturday, for both mothers so that Sunday would be free for my family and me.

"I'd like to invite you and Mary for a special Saturday brunch. I will have something like a high tea with both moms and the girls," I invited. "How does that sound?"

Not spending the entire day with Mother would be out of the ordinary. My high tea event had the special touches with a beautifully set table and food, and it took a lot of planning, but I knew it was worth it. The next day, Mother's Day, Leif and I took our girls up the shore for a hike, picnic, and family time. We shared many smiles and laughs, which made it a memorable day. I didn't call Mother that day. In the back of my mind, I knew I probably should, but I started to resist the "shoulds" of my life. At the forefront of my mind, I tried to set a healthy boundary. I might have pushed the envelope a little when we took a short detour that day. I don't recall any visits to my grandma's home for Mother's Day, but today it felt right to stop and visit her. When Mother found out that we had stopped to see her mother-in-law, her silence grew even quieter. I knew I had kicked the puppy. Not only had I resisted calling her, mostly out of stubbornness, but I had also offered well wishes to someone she didn't respect. The strength of my allegiances was being put to a test, and I was blatantly uncomfortable.

"I had honored both Mothers the day before and today was my day," said a quiet inner voice without much conviction.

..

Leif and I were dreamers. We were highly ambitious, goal-oriented partners with a vision not to be enslaved to debt or scarcity. H & L Investments was created as we started investing in real estate and rental units. We only had six rental units, but it kept us busy, and this side stream of income had the potential for significant future payoffs. A financial advisor looked over our numbers and returned with a favorable prognosis that included the words "financial freedom" and "millionaires." We weren't there yet, but that sure was validation to keep us focused and moving forward. Each real estate class and purchase took us one step closer to the future we were on fire to create.

To further support our real estate endeavor, I earned my Minnesota and Wisconsin realtor's licenses and hoped to bring in part-time income. Leif and I expected this career change to benefit our long-range goals and raise extra funds. In a different life, I might have enjoyed this career path. Unfortunately, a part-time realtor doesn't exist. The schedule was varied, and responsibilities changed depending on the market. It followed the rise and fall of the economy, which is not something I had previously paid attention to. Unluckily for me, I happened to join the force during the 2005-2010 real estate bust. I spent many unpaid moments comforting struggling sellers around a stagnant market. Buyers had an endless supply to look at with no rush to purchase. Being an independent real estate agent equated to many hours with varying payouts, and it was a difficult chapter in my life, lacking much balance.

We did utilize my license with our rental business, but not as much as we anticipated. Our family of four created a full schedule, and we maxed out our available time for property management. The mounting tension in our marriage and the spontaneous demands of a career in real estate was not a good fit. The intensity of home life was on an upward trajectory. As a realtor, I was essentially on the clock 24/7, and Leif hated that I might be called to jump into action without much notice. I tried to combine our summer family activities with a busy work season, but it left me stretched thin and only sometimes fully present. When the market's bleakness predicted no end, I stepped out of this career. I also had a secret hope that removing its inconsistency would alleviate some of the tension within the walls of our home.

..

Since Leif's parents lived next door and his Grandma lived up the road, family visits with coffee or a shared meal were commonplace. As a result, the girls grew up interacting with the three generations, usually with cousins nearby for playtime. Next door, Leif's mom, Mary, never seemed flustered, no matter how many adults and children were in her small country home. I fell in love with my mother-in-law for her easy going nature; she never placed guilt or shame on my shoulders and seemed to accept me. It felt so different from what I was used to.

On the other hand, there was always some tension between the three siblings. Both of Leif's sisters had strong personalities; sometimes, they would butt heads, yet other times they'd stand close to each other's side in unity. This crass form of communication was mind-blowing, as it seemed they could speak candidly to each other and later work through any fallout. It was organic. It made me wish we could have argued more when I was younger - or even now as an adult. How liberating it must feel to share your thoughts and feelings honestly!

I will be forever thankful for my glimpse of the loud auntie love that Leif's sisters showered on the nieces and nephews. The aunts had no problem running in for a monster hug or smothering the kiddos with affection. I didn't show those emotions so freely; I don't know if I even felt them. I watched my sisters-in-law modeling how to offer affection, and I stretched myself to be different. At first, it was something I had to force. It wasn't that I didn't feel love; instead, I didn't know how to show it. Then, as my walls came down, I felt great warmth and joy as I shared a greater openness with my nephews. It was a wonderful life lesson.

..

Leif had childhood friends with similar life paths that remained in the area after high school or college. The friends and their wives often gathered in a garage, around a bonfire, or at a table. The children played together and occupied themselves while the adults drank, played games, and socialized. My extroverted self had no problem serving as a host where I could control the environment, but I always felt uncomfortable going places with our daughters. We found a babysitter whenever it seemed appropriate. Typically, language and behaviors worsened as the night wore on, and I preferred the girls not to be there.

Looking back, this was a very close-knit group with solid friend-ships. Even though the women would regularly become frustrated with the behaviors of their men, there was an undercurrent of situational acceptance. Our culture club included excessive drinking, disrespect toward women, and a lack of concern for the young eyes taking it all in. Some husbands openly degraded women and suggested they were stu-pid, bitchy, or sex objects. On hunting ventures, the men would watch porn with younger boys in the room. Each couple had their own dance, not all were at a toxic level, but nobody was willing to make waves if they witnessed negative actions. Vulgarity was a currency.

When Leif was off from work, he started drinking shortly after noon, and his lazy pace of putting them back didn't conclude until bed-time. If we were with that friend group, my husband would receive un-spoken permission to celebrate even heartier, enjoying the bottomless beer. Like his dad's house next door, Blatz and Hamms were the cheap beer of choice. The two saved aluminum cans to sell for pennies on the pound at aluminum recycling centers. In hindsight, there shouldn't have been bragging rights for bringing truckloads of aluminum and making decent pocket money. Still, this wasn't a red flag for me.

Once Leif cracked the beer can and had consumed enough, his inhibitions melted away like sugar in the rain. No matter the crowd, he liked to talk about my body, sexuality, and even intimate things we had done. His monologue wasn't spoken confidently to a buddy; it was broadcast across the room. While insulting me, he often made eye contact. Was this a challenge? Did he consider this a compliment? No matter his motive, my feelings were always the same: mortification and embarrassment.

Regardless, people admired us for our life choices, beautiful daugh-ters, passion, and drive. Their constant amazement made it more dif-ficult for me to see that our relationship was unhealthy. By our sixth year of marriage, my motherly rampages about Leif's drinking were commonplace and regular. The sexual casualties were many. I accept-ed this as a part of the man I loved and the family I wanted to keep together. My value and self-worth were still not a factor in my choices, and it would be a bumpy road.

..

The girls attended our neighborhood charter school, so I was thrilled to accept a Title I Paraprofessional position after the real estate debacle. I tutored elementary students in reading and math. The first time I sat in a 6th-grade circle, I felt I had come home. Of course, these youngins weren't my normal-aged population, but their energy and innocence offered me a lot.

More importantly, I could stay within arm's reach of Michelle and Leila. Seeing the school in action was a gift; I knew when celebrations and conflicts might influence their world. Like when the school had a slight lice infestation, I had my finger on the pulse of what was being done to mitigate the nuisance (still, our household got it off and on for over three months). A favorite part of my job was organizing playground Olympics for the students during recess. My partner in crime, Carrie, and I made crazy obstacle courses, hid colored eggs around a double soccer field, and organized tetherball tournaments. After the multi-day adventures, we ended with awards or a hot chocolate party to celebrate. My work at this elementary school offered me much-needed joy in a world that seemed suffocating in darkness.

..

Leif got a vasectomy when he was only 25 years old, but we were confident that one more baby in the mix would be too much. There was plenty of drama within our marriage and family of four to last a lifetime. One year later, once the dust had settled and we had found our family's rhythm, we knew we had made a mistake.

"I think I want another baby. Did we make the wrong decision?" I cried.

Leif answered, "I don't know, Heather. I could see us with another baby. But do we really want to head down the road of a reversal?"

I shed a lot of tears, and we had plenty of discussions about our options. It wasn't an easy decision for the pocketbook, our egos, or his balls. Six months later, we made the 10k investment to have a vasectomy-reversal procedure down in the Cities at a specialized facility. Any man that wants nursing and hallmark-quality sympathy for a vasectomy should sit down with a man after he has had a reversal. It is not a gentle process. After a few months of healing, the doctor's follow-up concluded we should have no problem conceiving.

When the doctor gave the green light, we started trying for Stevens Baby #3. It had been around three years since I was last pregnant, and we both assumed this attempt would resemble the first two tries. As the months ticked by, there was no pregnancy. More doctor appointments were scheduled, primarily for me, and I had exploratory surgery (which only offered other issues like a spot on a kidney and a mass near my rectum!). Doctors had rechecked Leif's sperm count, and his results held no red flags. There wasn't a diagnosable reason we weren't conceiving naturally, so we moved on to stage two.

I started fertility drugs and shots, and when we still didn't conceive after a handful of months, my OB-GYN brought a state fertility specialist on board for artificial insemination. Our calendar for the next six months was micromanaged, like my body, trying to fertilize an egg with sperm. Our nurse asked us on multiple rounds if we were okay with twins since I had two or three viable eggs. Still, the result continued to be the same: no pregnancy. It just didn't make sense why all of our attempts were fruitless.

I felt guilty that I grieved our infertility. We had two beautiful, healthy girls already. Yet, I needed this baby to place a bandage over the gaping wound in my heart. After the unsuccessful sixth round, the specialist met with us to discuss our course.

He simply stated, "You have unexplained infertility."

He said this as if unexplained infertility had its own medical identity, like other ailments or diseases.

He really meant, "We don't know why you are not getting pregnant."

We had tried for almost four years, and it was time to accept the crossroad. Part of me felt deep relief to put it to rest; it had been a long haul. However, another part of me was so exhausted. I had to give up the wish that Baby #3 would be the secret formula to save our crumbling foundation.

..

Sometime around 2006 or 2007, in the middle of our infertility adventures, Leif decided he wanted to overcome his nicotine addiction. My dad had successfully done this with the help of a drug called Wellbutrin. Unfortunately, our insurance would not approve this specific medication but did allow the substitute drug Chantix. I had poked fun at the drug commercials with their long list of potential side effects, and I often wondered if any of these drugs carried benefits. Unfortunately, after only two weeks on Chantix, Leif had side effects from the medication. While my dad's mood had been uplifted and pleasant on Wellbutrin, Leif had an adverse reaction. His body had a more extreme version of nervous energy. He always had ongoing foot movements, which had served as the source for a tease. That jittery foot took on new life, and he admitted his emotions felt on edge and borderline uncontrollable.

"I hate feeling this way. I can't do it. So I am quitting this med," he said.

I comforted, "Of course, baby. It doesn't sound like it is going to help much if it makes you so agitated."

Quitting Chantix was the immediate solution, and the nicotine addiction seemed like the lesser of the two evils. He tried to remove this addiction from his system several times, but he had been using nicotine regularly since he was a young teen. If he wasn't smoking, he was chewing. When his chewing habit started to damage his lip or stomach (he swallowed and never spit), he switched back to smoking cigarettes. He had become an angry bear, and our family dealt with each attempt to quit. I wanted him to be successful and rid himself of the addiction, but I was starting to become nervous about who he turned into during his attempts. Eventually, I told him to give up his attempts to stop. The roller coaster was emotionally too tricky for all of us.

..

Seven years into our marriage with two children in tow, I constantly lived in a cloud of irritation and resentment. My snarky comments became more frequent toward Leif, especially about his disrespect or drinking. I was depressed. I knew my temper was shorter with the girls as I grappled for control of the life I had mapped out. I wasn't a mom who gave spankings; instead, I followed in the footsteps of Mother and became passive-aggressive. Silent treatments and cranky outbursts must have been a lot for the girls to process. The actual intended audience, Leif, wasn't persuaded into better actions with the negative spin on my mood.

Sometimes when I drove the girls down one of our many side dirt roads, I would lock up the brakes to get their attention. If they bickered in the backseat, I felt the rising tension and bristling in my chest and head. This anxiety felt like a million tiny needles pressing from the inside out, and I needed them to be quiet. So I slammed on the car breaks without notice and swung around in my seat to peer at them. As the dust settled outside, their startled eyes would meet mine.

"Stop arguing! I have had enough! Can we just get home in peace?" I demanded.

They didn't deserve my anger or my anxiety. I was so close to the edge that it didn't take much to send me flailing. Regrettably, the noise was one piece I was susceptible to. Michelle and Leila listened and remained quiet for the drive, probably hoping Momma would just keep her cool.

..

I don't know what demons my husband tried to drown out when he popped the top of the next beer; maybe he didn't know, either. On a few rare occasions of drunken' stupidity, Leif revealed hurts about a few different relationships within his family. Since we had built our home on his parent's gifted land, there was a constant presence as if our lives had merged into one. I struggled with that proximity. Having people walk into my home unannounced was very different for me. The only people that showed up unannounced at my parent's house were my grandparents, and I often heard how this made my mom feel disrespected. Sometimes I felt like George was the King, and Leif and I tried to reside within his kingdom. However, Leif didn't speak ill-mannered about his parents, he drank the same cheap beer as his old man, and I saw his silent submissiveness.

Our neighboring King soon made it apparent how much reign he had. Land and real estate continued to offer Leif and me both thrills of potential financial freedom, which we craved. We had a flux of money from a property sale and invested in a 20-acre parcel of raw land in Wisconsin. Somehow that parcel of land planted a seed for us to create a new homestead that offered a new chapter and distance from the close ties. It housed beautiful hardwood maples and oaks leading to a ridge overlooking a creek that would make an epic building site. We caught the building bug together - we put our heart, soul, and excitement into the plans for our new home. It would be a new life. The parcel was an equal distance from Leif's job, so it wasn't a huge change, yet we both knew it would be. It was a different state, zip code, and miles from family and friends. We rough-cleared a path for a driveway that led to the upcoming building site; this better defined our vision. One hundred thirteen wood ticks jumped from the woods onto our dogs and us in just one day of clearing. We hired a contractor to finish clearing and building the driveway. Later that summer, an architect was scheduled to take the blueprint design and make our dream home a reality. With the sale of our first home, we could make this transition without too much financial stress. It seemed like that plot of land in rural Wisconsin held our pot of gold at the end of the rainbow.

Leif was willing to break free from the North Shore grip and create a fresh start with me and the girls. I clung to the thought of this change and was subconsciously aware of the marital discord already happening in our current situation. Moving across state lines and starting over would improve our lives. However, I didn't understand how high the stakes were for us to create a fresh start.

On a balmy July 4th, we walked the field path to our neighbor's home. My in-laws sat on their deck, as they often did, relaxing under the shade of a nearby tree. We had not kept our relocation plans a secret, yet hadn't had an open conversation with King George. I am sure we were both nervous to talk to him; however, he wasn't readily available either and tended to keep to himself. On this day of independence, George was the one to speak up and start a conversation.

"I've heard about your plans for building on your new land," he started.

I sat next to Leif on the edge of the wooden boards of the deck, but I remember a space between us that I wanted to close. I intuitively knew we should be "joined" in unity, or maybe I felt compelled to remind him that WE had a plan.

"Well, your plans are fine. You two can do whatever you think is best. But if you move, I want the land back," George said.

Leif and I had been given those five acres as a wedding present. Together we had cleared every tree, built our home and garage, planted fruit trees, and made it a homestead. To give it back was utterly impossible. We needed to sell that ready-made home to the next excited family to transfer our sweat equity into our new home. If the plan didn't play out that way, there wouldn't be a new home. I don't remember the rest of the conversation with George that day or on any other. The ramifications of that short conversation were extensive, though. As we walked the path back to our own home, the weight of the message, its truth, came down upon us and our dreams. At first, it was such a shock that Leif and I hardly said anything to each other. Instead, we tried to stay positive and discussed alternative plans.

"What if we sold the house off the land, made some money, and then gave your dad back what he wants," I said.

That wouldn't make enough money for us.

Leif offered, "What if we remove this home and build our dream home on this site? We already have the yard and garage done."

That idea lasted a little longer but also fell into the black abyss. We were pushing ideas to build our dream home, but the real problem was not the walls and roof where we resided. What we really needed was a whole new restart where the habits and trends of the people around us wouldn't influence our happiness. At least, that was my dream.

I may have walked home with my husband on that memorable day in July, but who held rein in our family's choices was evident. We only discussed the move again for minor details that we needed to put to rest. We canceled the clearing and driveway construction and angered the professional that worked on our blueprints. I was amazed George could crush our vision with only a few sentences while sitting on his back deck, casually sipping his Blatz.

..

George was a man of few words and even fewer emotions. He had some losses early in life and even went off the continent for a year to work when Leif and his sisters were young. George was a modern-day Walden, alone in the woods, without the transcendental ponderings. Midway through our marriage, we had two labradors that were Leif's hunting dogs. Maggie was his well-aged chocolate lab and lived an easy life between the two neighboring homes, and Sandy was the yellow lab that had recently learned the hunting ropes. One pheasant hunting fall, Maggie struggled with declining health and wasn't strong enough for the aggressive workouts in the South and North Dakota fields. Leif took Sandy to the Dakotas and left Maggie in my care. We didn't necessarily believe she was on death's door, but everyone kept an eye on her. She went missing for an extended time (even though she was free to roam next door and into the woods), so I asked next door if they had seen her. My father-in-law arrived at my slider door, and I repeated my inquiry. George, with red eyes, told me that she was gone.

"She died? Did you find her in the woods?" I choked out.

With a slight shake of his head, I realized what he meant. He had "taken care" of Maggie. Real men believed they could take their pet back, shoot it, and be emotionally okay. I cannot say whether or not George struggled with what he did; but to him, he had shot Maggie to put her out of her misery. I cried tears and felt immense sympathy for George. We shared a rare hug. After he left, I was alone to deal with my thoughts; I started to feel uneasy about the whole situation. My husband would come home in a few days to learn that his dad had ended his dog's life without talking to him first. George had put down Leif's dog without an opportunity for him to say goodbye. He thought this was easier for Leif not to make the decision, but I couldn't help wondering if he had the right to make that choice.

A couple of days later, when Leif returned, George wasn't nearby to tell his son the news. I had to look my husband in the eye and tell him his Maggie Girl was gone. Leif grieved the dog's passing, yet I don't remember any emotional reaction to his dad's actions. I can be almost certain he didn't confront his dad.

..

It was a typical summer weekend out at a local Minnesota lake, and we had planned a day visit with our North Shore group of friends. The girls were with us, and we had no intention of spending the night. Once we arrived, we stopped by an older generation's campsite to visit. Three generations were milling around - from the more aging parents, our friends, and all the next-generation children. Michelle and Leila were about five and four and loved playing with their neighborhood friends. There were a lot of kiddos in this age group, with the oldest boys being seven. They had grown up together, and these kids had strong friendships.

Just another casual conversation around the firepit turned gross and set the tone for the rest of the day.

A grandpa looked at his seven-year-old grandson and asked, "So when are you going to mount her?"

"Her" was referring to our precious, blond-curled five-year-old, Michelle. I had always considered this older man a puke, but he also scared me, and I didn't trust his mouth or temper. Of the many people who sat around the campfire in lawn chairs, I don't remember anyone correcting him unless his wife gave a nervous laugh and told him to knock it off. Russ was just like that. To add a shine to this morning, Russ also gave me the public nickname "Hot Tits." Writer and film producer Stephen Chbosky is screaming in my head, now removed from this nightmare by 15 years, "We accept the love we think we deserve."

My husband didn't stand up for me, but the words that typically came out of his mouth (when under the influence) weren't all that different. He revered the local men of this generation; they could do no wrong, and he seemed to crave acceptance by their group. I would love to say that these words were the worst of the day, but that would be lying. Russ called me Hot Tits all day; I uncomfortably accepted the insults while Leif laughed and drank with everyone. As afternoon turned to evening, it was no surprise he didn't want to leave. The pressure was high around the bonfire, as everyone wanted us to stay. It would be a long, late-night drive for me with a wasted husband and the girls; neither offer seemed very pleasant. Eventually, someone offered a tent and bags, and it was clear we would stay.

On this night, the sounds and words that floated into the tent where I lay with our two girls should not have been spoken nor heard. Russ and Leif were the last two drunks at the campfire, and they continued to sling them back. At one point, their conversation turned to the topic of Hot Tits.

"So tell me, does she have nice tits?"

No pause was offered from my husband before he answered, "Fuck, no."

"We accept the love we think we deserve."

"We accept the love we think we deserve."

"We accept the love we think we deserve."

I don't know where the conversation went from there. Did Leif and Russ laugh, or maybe they shrugged in disappointment that my tits weren't all that hot after all. It doesn't matter what was said next because I didn't hear it. Some say that alcohol can be a truth serum, and that truth really hurts. It was common for Leif to talk about my body in degrading ways. It was also customary for him to share intimate details

around the glow of a campfire with anyone that would listen. This one stung differently. He didn't think I was beautiful or sexy.

I returned to their conversation in time to hear my inebriated husband get lippy with this generational clan master. It was like the golden retriever felt brave with the pit bull.

I don't know what Leif said to aggravate the pit, but the dominant dog put the small fry back in his place, "Watch it, boy, or I will go into that tent, grab your kids, boil, skin, and eat them."

I stopped breathing. I wanted to vomit. I wanted to cry, scream, and bash my fists into both men's faces. Another option was to wake my little loves, carry them to the car, and drive away, never to return. I froze in agony and fear, which was the worst thing to do.

How? How can a human come up with that threat? How the fuck does a father hear that and not throw that poor excuse-for-a-man into the fire? How did I not run? Like so many other times in my life, I had no voice. I believed Leif was the love of my life, and my happiness depended on keeping this family together. My instincts to protect my daughters from these horrible humans were not strong enough to fight back. I don't remember if I talked to Leif about it the next day. I assume I did. It probably sounded like the other times I reminded him of his actions the night before: peeing in the corner of our bedroom, unzipping his pants in front of family, or talking about my body like I was the next porn queen.

All he could say was, "I was drunk."

That night, I allowed this man to crawl into the tent next to me. He laid down in a drunken slump and fell into his typical sleep with snores and chokes. He laid down only inches from his daughters. I stared at the tent walls and felt them close in, suffocating me. The next day we got into our vehicle and drove home together because we were a family.

..

After the birth of our two daughters, I felt like I had lost control of the shape of my body. I tried fad diets, but I needed something more aggressive. To maintain my husband's interest, I was obsessed with staying youthful and sexy and restoring my appearance. Athletics and I had never coexisted for long besides aerobics and walking excursions. Leif was also interested in toning up after inching into middle age. We figured running was easy enough, not needing too much equipment, and decided to prepare for a 5k race. Near the end of winter, when the roads were not ready to tackle, we stood in the living room and ran in place, thinking some activity was better than no activity. When the ice melted and the roads dried, I took my inaugural run outside with a barely adequate sports bra and bulky, hulkish tennis shoes; I almost died and seriously considered my sanity for signing up for a race. Physical fitness had never been a big part of my life, and my weight had managed itself accordingly. Unfortunately, that wasn't my body story any longer. So, desperate times call for desperate measures; I bought new sports bras and a pair of running shoes and tried again.

I celebrated when I successfully ran one mile and then two without stopping! I didn't say it was a pretty celebration, as I usually hit the end of the run heaving from over-exertion. But pushing myself outside my comfort zone was empowering, and I wanted more! My body started responding to the increase in activity, and I started feeling better about my reflection in the mirror. Finally, we made it to race day, and my husband and I ran the Grandma's Marathon 5k; I had so much adrenaline that I threw in a 200-yard sprint to the finish line. That sense of accomplishment and worthiness was exhilarating and addictive. I finally had control of something in my life.

I pushed harder and longer to achieve more in the running wheelhouse. A new chapter opened up to five years of dedicated training plans, 5ks, half marathons, and an extensive collection of race t-shirts. No distance seemed too far, and I added the completion of a full marathon to my bucket list.

..

Leif and I never struggled to keep the fires burning in the bedroom. Whether I was actually interested in our daily intimacy or leaning into codependent behavior to keep him happy was a gray area. When Leif told me his coworker thought I was sexy, I was flattered. That flirtatious banter rolled right into our playful banter behind closed doors. Both of us had noticeably toned our bodies with so much running and increased exercise, so it felt only natural to also feel friskier.

Our playful chatter seemed to take on new life as we started regularly hanging out and partying with Leif's coworkers at the bar. Everyone was loose and fancy-free. Sometimes the flirting felt like we were pushing limits, yet when we went home from the bar, those interactions wove into Leif and my intimate conversations. It seemed like no harm, no foul. At another gathering, the suggestive bantering got more direct and intense. Leif's coworker wanted to show us the new construction progress on his first home a few miles away. I felt nervous energy coursing through my veins, even though I couldn't pinpoint why. The three of us toured his house, walking room to room, yet the tour paused at the top of the stairs.

Why or how it started, I don't remember. Neither guy acknowledged the tears as they rolled down my face. I was under the influence but still perfectly coherent - I just didn't speak up or change the course of action. How had playful fantasies voiced at home led us to this point?

Waves of shame washed over me; I cherished my husband, yet I couldn't rationalize what had happened. Along with the guilt, I also felt a deep sadness. Our vows mentioned love, honor, and protection but never said anything about sharing.

"We accept the love we think we deserve."

..

While my life was filled with doctoring, an angry husband, and emotional overload, my relationship with Mother was also declining. However, this time felt slightly different because I also felt agitated and resentful. So many parts of my life were out of balance; the unnecessary drama that seemed to be worn like a badge of honor was just too much. So I started playing a new emotional game with her. At a women's scrapbooking retreat, I purposefully picked a spot across the room from her to create for the weekend. One part of me didn't believe we had to sit side by side in a room full of friends, while the other part knew this would seriously wound her. I stubbornly wouldn't give her what she wanted and tried to create a new space for myself until her passive-aggressive rebuttal had me returning to her to fix the damage.

Around this time, an aunt was getting a divorce from my uncle. Many family members reached out to support her. I took some tearful walks with her and offered an ear and shoulder. She started giving me the same in return as the need to release pent-up emotions around my quickly-changing marriage.

This newfound friendship with my aunt bothered my parents. Our deeper bond caught them off guard, which had Julie reaching out to them less often. Jealousies popped up, and Mother would comment about how often we were together.

"Why have you been with Julie so much lately? She doesn't even call us anymore for support," Mother said.

I answered, "I have been helping her. She needs comfort, and I am available. There isn't anything wrong with it. If you want to talk to her, you are welcome to call her."

The more Mother pushed this topic, the more defensive I got. I resisted. I didn't think I needed to change how much I was around my aunt. The tension mounted as the battle over Heather's loyalties reached a pinnacle behind the scenes.

Mother sent Julie (her sister-in-law) an email and accused her of stealing my attention. She made statements about Julie's relationships with her three children and ended it with, "You are dead to me."

Both Julie and I felt wrung out, so we parted ways to allow more space for Mother.

..

Eight years into my marriage, I realized it wasn't all white picket fences. With Leif's intense need for control, he obsessed about the pieces of my past. He questioned items I had kept over the years, people I talked about, and others I didn't mention. In his eyes, it all pointed toward guilt. So to quiet his demons, I eliminated pieces of my history - from old yearbook entries, high school projects that mentioned former boyfriends, prom photos--anything that was a memory of my earlier years on the planet. If I didn't comply or if I argued their worth, I was asking for a fight.

"Why would you need to keep that? Can't you let go? I can't believe you still have that prom picture with your high school boyfriend," he growled.

He'd accuse me that I still loved those men—all of them. Now the prom pictures I have left are of me standing alone in my pink dress or a group of girlfriends. I ripped out pages in my yearbook because of what my friends had written over 15 years before. My identity and purpose were to bend, adapt, and abide by whatever this man wanted or accept his accusations of my betrayal. I loved my husband and would do ANYTHING to prove my love to him. I was willing to relinquish any parts of myself to help him feel more secure.

When his demands became more insistent and persistent, I had the ah-ha moment that I wasn't in charge of our family. I honestly believed I was the household manager and "leader" since I tended to make responsible decisions. I might have been those things, but that didn't mean my thoughts and feelings were the final votes. With Leif, I worked so hard to maintain control and order and to keep him happy, yet I couldn't persuade him to "do the right thing." My expectations of what a functioning family should resemble kept getting kicked to the curb over and over.

That was the basis of our relationship: mother and child. I was the one who wanted to follow a rigid moral compass; he was the one that wanted to push limits. My new realization formed a wad of fear in my chest, and understanding I couldn't control him put a new lens in place. When would he choose a healthier life if I had no control? When would he see how much his actions and public perversions crushed my soul? I was terrified because I saw no change or end in sight. I stared into the mirror of my forever, and my hope that things would change was very bleak.

I knew my love for him had changed when I started celebrating his leaving for his outdoor adventures. I didn't care anymore; life was easier when he wasn't around.

There were no eggshells, and nobody questioned my integrity. While he was gone on one of his hunting trips, I chatted with a friend.

"Heather, have you gotten on Facebook yet? I am so addicted to one of their word games," she said. "You should try it."

In 2008, I still needed to get into social media as the various platforms were relatively new. There were more hunting trips in the fall, and I knew I would have a fair amount of extra time on my hands; a word game sounded rather entertaining and mind-numbing. I was, after all, an English teacher at heart. So I created my first Facebook account at age 33, found the word game, and binged the escape. As an official FB member, I explored what this mega-trend offered. I saw people like local friends, family, and coworkers with their profiles and quickly hit "Add Friend." I tracked down former friends, long-distance acquaintances, and even a foreign exchange student in Sweden that I hadn't thought of since I was 18. The discovery was fabulous fun. I typed anyone's name from my sphere of influence to see if I could find them and sneak a peak. I even typed in old boyfriends' names for curiosity's sake. I felt more alive and connected than I had in a long time.

..

It's a random date, but for me, it stands out. It was November 26, 2008, the night before Thanksgiving. Leif had spent parts of the previous month on his hunting trips to the Dakotas; meanwhile, I found time to craft and explore Facebook. Later at night, our phone rang.

"HEATHHHHHER! It's John, and I am out with Sarah at the Legion! Come join us! We want to see you!" my friend's voice boomed into the phone.

I laughed, "Oh, it's great to hear from you! No, no. I am already heading to bed. You two can have some fun for me."

We spent a few minutes catching up, and I mentioned, "I just tried to find you on Facebook!"

He told me he wasn't a member. We shared a few more pleasantries before hanging up. Moments earlier, Leif had flipped back the covers on the bed and stormed out of the bedroom. After ending the call, I walked out to explore.

I found a very livid husband pacing the room.

"What? Are you mad John called?" I asked somewhat defiantly. "I wasn't interested in going out. You heard me."

"Why were you searching for him on Facebook? Are you trying to hook up with him?" he accused.

"John?" I laughed. "He has always been a friend. No, I connected with many classmates on Facebook the past two weeks."

His anger seemed so off-base and excessive, and I fought back. I was sick and tired of his overreacting and aggression which accused me of wrongdoing.

"Just because I was looking up a male high school friend does not make me a cheater!" I shouted.

No matter how I voiced my defense, there was no reasoning with the man in front of me. This fight wasn't like any other we'd had before in eight years of marriage. Instead, this next chapter of our relationship was shrouded in fear with around-the-clock defenses against numerous accusations. This chapter lasted for the final 43 months of our marriage.

I was naive to the heightened change in our marriage. There was an unease between us after the Thanksgiving argument. His anger did not just blow over; I could sense a new level of tension, along with my mounting frustrations and resentment. At a friend's gathering, I threw digs at Leif about the Facebook charade as we sat around the table chatting. Almost everyone there was already on FB (men and women alike) and did vouch that people connect on this platform.

I asserted, "Hey! You are on Facebook! Do you have old classmates as friends there? Even if they are the opposite sex?"

I openly badgered Leif's attitude and lack of understanding, hoping to muster enough votes in my corner. But unfortunately, that discussion only made him feel ganged up on and fueled his anger toward me, no matter how many agreed that social media friendships and connections could be platonic. It still had been the wrong move for Heather.

The next few months did not help my case with Leif, and the perfect storm let loose its gale forces. I had a stroke of bad luck and poor choices to round out 2008, although there was more brewing down our dead-end country road.

The second event that solidified my judgment as the "cheater" was the Twin Ports Realtor Christmas party at the Duluth Entertainment Convention Center. This polished event is the highlight of the year for area realtors, with well-dressed professionals showing up to mingle. The holiday decorations were a lovely accent that complemented the view of the panoramic windows that looked over our port's Lift Bridge. This group of coworkers had become my friends, and I had a wonderful evening celebrating the holiday season with them. I felt glamorous in my black velvet camisole top and organza skirt in metallic swirls of black, gold, and turquoise. We had a delicious meal, drank wine, conversed, and laughed heartily. The evening entertainment featured dancing, and I eagerly moved to the dance floor; I loved dancing's energy, freedom, and self-expression. This night was no different. This night Leif didn't grace the dance floor but stood on the sidelines with the other disinterested spouses. While the effects of the wine took hold, I danced with Bob. He was a much older gentleman coworker who also loved to dance. We cut a rug and had a wonderful time.

It was my Christmas party, and I argued I needed an evening to cut loose. Our Thanksgiving episode was fresh and raw; I wanted a night to be numb.

"How could you? You were all over Bob on the dance floor last night! I stood right next to Kelly and watched! It was sickening!" Leif ranted.

My heart dropped and a pit formed in my stomach. Our marriage was in such a tough spot, yet I had flirted with another man publicly. Leif was thoroughly pissed off, and anger rolled off him in waves. I had no leg to stand on, as I couldn't remember the details very well.

"I am so sorry! You know I am not interested in Bob," I cried. "He is over 20 years older than me and happily married!"

My apology fell on deaf ears, and my thoughts raced about what my coworkers must be thinking about me. What if Bob's wife hated me?

"Leif, I only have eyes for you," I pleaded.

What wife would make her husband question her loyalty twice in one month? I did call Bob soon after to test the waters and see if there were any residual issues I needed to smooth. Everything in our conversation was lighthearted, as he mentioned how much fun he had at the party. At least it didn't seem like he had been offended and didn't say anything about his wife. Unfortunately, his casualness didn't offer me peace because it was his word against Leif's.

Less than one month later, his name came across my cell phone, and my husband saw red.

"Why is he calling you?" he raged.

He was confident that I was having an affair, and my heart trembled. I saw no other option than to permanently end the friendship with Bob to make peace with Leif. Unfortunately, I didn't know how to explain my new distance, so I ghosted my coworker and friend. It was what I needed to fix the mess within my home.

We had another bone-chilling fight at our favorite resort. I desperately wanted the new year to arrive as it would clean the slate for our marriage. I needed life to be less traumatic and wished for a magical New Year's Eve to solve it. That didn't happen.

On this holiday away, at the end of 2008, Leif had been using our laptop with my dad. When he typed in the search bar, it showed previous historical searches, including the names I had entered in my Facebook search. It also included my ex-fiance and high school boyfriend amongst the 100+ other people I had searched.

"I have no interest in anyone else! I swear!"

"I wasn't trying to contact them."

"This is how Facebook works. I searched out everyone I could think of, like a game."

"I wasn't cyberstalking my ex. No! I have no interest in any of them! I didn't even friend-request a single one!"

His anger was off the charts as he paced around the resort bedroom. As I faced his disgust and rage, no calming, explaining, or reasoning found footing with my words and pleas. I suffocated in the quicksand hole I had created. Fear danced with panic as I tried to understand my actions, "Why did I keep incriminating myself?" These episodes kept stacking up, and the guilt consumed me. That New Year, there wasn't much of a celebration when Liz & Joe joined us at the cabin. Instead, I was a wounded, out-of-place, poor excuse for a wife with no roadmap to set my marriage back on track. Now I needed to figure out why I kept screwing up.

..

I invite you to the part of my life that gets muddier. There are both celebratory and toxic events, yet they blend without order. For the next few years, I simply survived, and I didn't retain some of the most simple details, yet I hold powerful memories I would love to forget. I guess that is how trauma works.

My uncle passed away in the fall of 2009. It was unexpected and caught our extended family off guard. Leif and I attended his celebration of life and then joined the mourners an hour away at my uncle's favorite bar. After an emotional day, nothing sounded better than unwinding with a beer and family. The overall family dynamics remained uncomfortable, so my parents declined to join, releasing one level of tension from the day.

At first, the gathering in the local bar was an excellent decompression from the intense day. As the evening wore on, the alcohol calmed nerves, and family interactions relaxed and enjoyable with plenty of storytelling. But, as with many events centered around alcohol, the energy started to change. The pendulum moved off the peaceful center, and people's sorrows returned. I found myself at a table with relatives, discussing my parents.

"Why didn't they come here with the rest of us? Are they too good to come to a bar?" one aunt asked.

"I bet Shirley wouldn't let your dad come. He would have wanted to be here," another added.

My tongue loosened, and I shared the heavy baggage I carried.

"They don't like to be around Julie and me," I explained. "Our close relationship makes them uncomfortable."

Validation didn't come my way very often when it came to the calamity circling the relationship with my parents. Having the attention of family at the table resembled support, but I walked a delicate line. It was true; the struggle with Mother for over five years wasn't something I could hide anymore, especially since the more immediate unrest with Leif took most of my energy. However, as the stories morphed away from memories of my uncle and strictly to the angst felt toward my parents, I quickly became overwhelmed. Conversations were no longer about me and my struggles; they became about everyone else and their inner aggressions toward Mother.

I was torn, as a part of me wanted to hear these juicy stories my parents had sheltered from me. I held the key to a vault of information, but I couldn't decide if I wanted to use it. Their verbal diarrhea came at me from all sides. It was too much - my emotions were too strung out and fragile to support them. Not only that, it wasn't my job. I didn't want to defend my parents, yet I couldn't sit there nodding my head, either. For the rest of the evening, I wandered from bar corner to corner, searching for a safe place to land away from the toxic sludge many offered.

That night opened my eyes to the other side of the family's rumblings. For years, I had heard one side of the story, and now that I had a glimpse at the other, I cannot say I regretted being in the dark. I landed in the messy middle, and I didn't know if I had to choose a side, ignore it, or feel resentful. At the night's end, I got into the car with my husband and drove home, hoping to leave it all behind.

..

For the next few years, I was busy putting bandages and gauze tape over the all-out hemorrhage of my marriage and family. My guilt and his anger manifested a level of anxiety I had never experienced. I was jumpy and edgy, and my mind ran a race with no finish line. Quicksand met eggshells as I lived with a stranger; I didn't know how I had sunk this deep or how to get out. Naively, my love for Leif was still solid, and I never considered leaving. I believed living a life of constant fear and resentment was just the way it was going to be until he changed or got healthier. Then, while out to dinner with a girlfriend, she suggested I leave him.

"Heather, maybe it is time to think about leaving Leif. Your stress is so high. I don't think he is treating you all that well."

I felt aggravated with her for even suggesting that. Couldn't she just be here to listen to me?

"No, that isn't an option. I love him," I said. "If he slowed his drinking, we would be fine."

Her final comment, "Do you really think he will do that?"

I didn't like or respect my husband anymore, but I focused on repairing, not leaving. Staying married was a dream I held tightly: if I tried harder, loved bigger, or sacrificed more, he would finally be happy again and see my pure love for him. If he would lessen his drinking, trust his wife to be faithful, or maybe get some medical help, we could get back on track.

The educator in me tried to demonstrate how humans could allow alcohol into their life in healthier habits. Sometimes I leaned into my religious upbringing and tried to be alcohol-free and still fun. I also auditioned as the poster child for healthy alcohol moderation, wearing a halo while holding a glass of wine. But, just as many times, I threw in the towel and joined him. No matter which hat I wore, the same version of Leif showed up at the party.

On the occasions I simply chose to join him, there wasn't someone operating the ship and keeping us safe. After one night with both of us partying, we walked to the car, determining who was sober enough to drive us the 40 minutes home.

"How do you feel? Can you drive?" I asked.

Whenever I drank, I handed over complete trust and discernment to anyone other than myself. It's just what I did, and I already had predicted his answer.

"Give me the keys. I am fine to drive," Leif answered.

As he drove us home, racing 100 MPH in my Ford Taurus down Hwy 61, Leif shared, "I am closing one eye."

"Why would you do that?" I asked.

"So I don't see four different lanes," he answered.

We made it home, but our little girls easily could have been orphans with one butterfly effect moment.

..

I searched for the magic formula that would get us back to our peaceful life. Unfortunately, I ran out of options to try—my magic wand shot blanks. Our world had morphed into a rhythm where he significantly drank at home; there was a constant battle for control, with plenty of anger and accusations. I considered myself lucky he wasn't someone that enjoyed the bar as if that vindicated him from his issue with alcohol. Ultimately, I didn't trust him out of my sight. Who was going to keep watch or tell him he couldn't drive? That was about the only thing I could control. He had no problem drinking and driving and went into the ditch more than once during our marriage. Hell, he would open a beer while we drove anywhere local, including when the girls were in the car. This wasn't a fight I could win, so I learned to watch his level of intoxication with microscopic precision.

In a church pew, he leaned over and whispered that the man in front was the guy that had tried to help in the ditch. This local had tried to help a stranded driver on this winter night until he sensed the driver might be intoxicated.

The good Samaritan asked, "Are you drunk?"

Leif retorted, "Fuck you."

The man left the scene, and Leif had to figure out his ditch mess. Here was the reminder that stared at him from within our local church. I don't know if he felt any shame from this incident. It didn't stop him from drinking and driving, so any possible guilt is irrelevant.

I didn't trust him around other women either. To some extent, it was because of the perversion he demonstrated right in front of me. It was also the things he said or did when he thought I wasn't looking. I had a love/hate relationship with our friend group because these gatherings seemed to bring out the worst in him. The ladies were my closest friends, and I knew their husbands well. We would eat good food, play games, laugh, and drink. Many times the evening came to a close with some intense drama between Leif and me, whether about his level of intoxication, choosing to go home, or some perversion voiced. I didn't like who I had become when we socialized; I felt like a hawk, watchful and calculating. That is where I messed up; I was NEVER able to control anything around Leif's drinking, and if I had just given up the need to control, maybe I would have seen the truth in front of my eyes. Unfortunately, I couldn't and wouldn't give up hope that this man would forgive me for my missteps and love me again.

..

Journal Entry - December 26, 2010

I don't want to be the victim any longer. I don't want to be accused of things I didn't do. I don't want to be the source of his anger when all I've been is committed. It's not fair. I don't want to be worried about him drinking and driving. Maybe for once I'd like an escape from the pain. But I don't run & I don't medicate with booze - so here I sit. I don't want to talk to anyone - I just want to pray. Lead me. Heal my hurts. Help me keep calm with my kids. They deserve stability & safety.

..

Our friend group was on a snowmobile trip at the Gunflint hills, one of the most beautiful places to ride. I don't remember the specific order of events on this trip, but the highlights can be summarized into three critical moments: the snowmobile accident, the flirting, and my long walk. That is a strange combination of memories to come from a remote snowmobile trip. A large group of us reserved a cabin on a lake for a long weekend, and we had access to riding outside the door. I didn't have a sled and never really had the desire, so I usually rode with a girlfriend. As everyone gathered on the lake to begin the day ride, some of our riders warmed up, darting across the icy playground. A vast open space is a calling card for speed and snowmobiles. I turned around to watch Leif.

Just as my eyes focused on him, his snowmobile launched up a pressure ridge, and his body hung suspended in the air in an awkward pose. Gravity took over and brought the sled and its driver down to the ground. From our viewpoint, there was only minor damage as the sled kept driving forward, Leif still the occupant. His helmet cracked, and his leg hurt, but he insisted we continue with our planned day of trail riding. It wasn't forty-five minutes later when his handlebars fell off. His leg had hit them so hard that it had sheared the metal supports. Our fun did end shortly for the day (and trip) as we towed his sled back to the resort.

Oh, he was in pain. As his adrenaline started to wear off, the pain in his thigh intensified. I don't remember if any of us suggested that he drive to a doctor or hospital, but he didn't. Instead, he just opened another beer. I was uncomfortable with the day and the direction of the night, and I remained sober while the others enjoyed the eve. The party wore on, and I was ready to call it a night. Leif was exceptionally drunk at this point and offered a placating response that he would join me shortly.

When he didn't join me for bed, I couldn't stop listening to the continued shenanigans from the other room. I stared out the bedroom door, hoping he would see me and get the hint. After recently losing weight, I purchased a prettier nightie for our rustic trip, hoping to get my man excited. Unfortunately, that romantic scenario I had played out wasn't happening. Instead, my attempts became more passive-aggressive as I spied from the doorway before launching myself back onto the creaky bed. Back and forth, up and down, with the same result from both my husband and me. The more I watched, the more anxious and panicky I became. Now, my man and a younger, beautiful friend flirted openly. I saw the chemistry between them, and I didn't like it. As I tried to sleep, I remained voiceless and frozen.

I woke up angry and hurt beyond measure as I stared at his sleeping figure next to me. My skin and brain bristled from the lack of sleep and the over-abundance of anxiety. This morning was typical in the saga of my marriage, but I needed just to get away from it all today. So I got up before everyone else, put on my winter layers, and left. I walked all damn morning, and only the still of the Gunflint Hills could compete with the raging banshee in my head. I walked down a winding, snow-covered remote road and stopped at a boat launch that led out to a frozen lake. I paused, breathed in the chilly air, and was thankful it wasn't too windy. On my long winter walk, I didn't ponder how to restore my life or marriage; I purposely avoided that cabin as a message to everyone else.

My numb emotions encouraged, "Be the victim. Let them know how awful this situation feels."

I wanted to be that lost girl who walked the back country roads in winter for hours to receive attention and validation for how much I hurt. Someone could sit down and soothe my wounds. Or someone could sit down with my husband and tell him to open his eyes to the results of his actions. Five hours later, I returned to the cabin, and the response I longed for differed from what I received. As I walked into the place I had left before anyone was even out of bed, I found it alive with movement, games, and everyday life. Nobody's world halted on my behalf, and nobody even mentioned my being gone for hours. Leif wasn't concerned; my girlfriends didn't come to my emotional rescue. Everyone treated me like I had stepped outside simply to grab an armload of wood. Their response reinforced my feelings of self-worth; it didn't matter. My pain didn't matter.

Life continued. The two-hour drive home was another episode featuring the mother scolding her child as he nodded his head and promised he'd do better. Those promises would be broken within days, with hardly a remembrance of the words he had spoken.

..

Our life's cadence revolved around the themes of my promiscuity and the need to be a better woman and wife.

My shirts were too revealing. No, I didn't purposely bend over to reveal my boobs. No, I didn't want to live in turtlenecks.

Leif thought Bella in Twilight was a two-timing manipulator. If I liked the books, I must think it is okay to send mixed messages to two guys! His insistence on this was so intense I declined to go to the movie with friends.

I mentioned that male teacher too many times. No, I don't fantasize about him!

I didn't introduce you to that male janitor? Yes, I also saw his exposed abs when he reached to change that lightbulb. No, that didn't make me crave his body.!

A male coworker needed a ride to the car dealership after a teaching day. That made you furious? Ok, I will awkwardly refuse to do it again next week when he asks.

Yes, I do have to have a work email. We have a joint one, but I have to use the one at school. I promise I am not doing anything I shouldn't.

On our Mexico vacation, I didn't mind that you went to the bar every night while I had to stay in the room with the girls. Although I would have preferred you stayed with me.

Yes, that was my ex-fiance in my parent's 25th wedding anniversary VHS tape. My parents don't hate you, and I don't want him back. I can ask them not to show it again.

Yes, my dad worked with John's dad. I am sorry he brought up his name, even though we were great friends in high school. No, I never fucked him.

Why did I say "Hi" to those two older people? They were Tommy's parents, and I wasn't going to be rude. No, I didn't think it was necessary to introduce you.

I have gone to counseling for myself, but I would really like us to go together.

Yes, life is easier when you are either passed out or gone.

Yes, that was me crying in the shower.

Yes, I feel scared and powerless.

Yes, I feel hunted.

No, I don't know what to do.

My life wasn't my own anymore. I yearned for any living soul to step in and tell me I had permission to leave. It took me a long time to come to the understanding that nobody was going to rescue me. I looked around my carefully laid out world - the home we built, the dreams we shared - and I tried to imagine my life if I'd walk away from it and only have the girls fifty percent of the time. I didn't even have a full-time job in place to support myself. It just was not an option to leave.

..

I had been living a nightmare for almost two years. My eyes and soul resembled a cornered, partially mangled rabbit that felt its imminent doom. I shot arrows in the dark and hoped to hit the board and find a reprieve from the intensity of daily life. I wanted the winds to switch, even slightly. Let me breathe.

I counted on the strength of my church family during this time. By this point in our marriage, Leif no longer had an interest in attending. I found a church I connected with and regularly brought the girls. The more invested I became, the more my spiritual awareness increased. I was thankful for this space without the pressure from my husband.

"HOLY! There you are! Welcome to the party," my spirit guides bellowed out during a church book study.

I was a shell of my former self. The abuse had gone on for two years, and I was utterly lost. I didn't have a plan, path, or inner peace. We read *The Big and Beautiful God* by James Bryan Smith for the study. The core message allowed me to understand my narratives about a higher power. I learned my narratives about God mirrored the expectations I felt from the essential people in my life. They (Mother, Dad, Leif, friends, and God) felt disappointed when I let them down. Yet, if I "tried harder" and "did better," I earned the love I craved. This class allowed me to analyze my beliefs about my worthiness, life purpose, and methods to receive love. My reality exploded when the book study leader asked us to listen in prayer rather than to make requests. I had never considered listening during prayer, nor had it been suggested in my decades with organized religion.

As soon as I closed my eyes and tried to tune in, a higher power started chanting in my head, "Let him go. Let him go. Let him go."

I never, ever heard anything while praying, and this was how it was going to start? These three words echoed, and I cried silently and sat on the cold leather couch. I couldn't ignore the message; it was insistent. It cracked me open a little. I didn't take action, but I wasn't ready to stop listening.

..

With emotions out of control, one thing I could do was hit the pavement. Exercise and running had a way of blocking out some of my harsh realities. Maybe if I sweat enough, it would decrease the amount of water that flowed from my eyes on a daily basis. With numerous 5ks and half marathons under my belt, all I could do was push harder and further. In 2010, I signed up for Grandma's Marathon; I was ready to tackle the 26.2 mile beast. The training required great focus - dieting, hydrating, cross-training, and monitoring. During those seven months of preparation, I was driven and focused; I needed this brain and body space.

At the marathon's starting line, I returned to my childhood memories when the TV helicopters circled over our house for the race and captured footage. I could never have predicted that I would someday stand at that starting line, less than a mile from my bedroom window. I paced well for the race as I did a walk/run rotation. I met a soul sister at mile six, and we continued for the remaining 16 miles. Along the way, we started with small talk. Still, as the miles continued and our energy waned, our discussions deepened into more profound stories about our partners, infertility, and broken body images. Finally, at mile 22, when I saw my daughters hold up "Go, MOM" signs, all I could do was cry. I had to finish this damn race!

I crossed that finish line waving my arms in the air, using the last of my reserves. My goal had been to finish in 5:30, and I managed 5:31. I had slowed some the last six miles, cheering on my new running buddy. In my mind, I had met all my goals and cried tears of relief. My recovery post-race was relatively smooth, and I even remembered feeling worse after some half-marathons. I wore that medal around my neck until my head hit the pillow that night, thankful that my body carried me on that colossal run along the shore of beautiful Lake Superior before ending in Canal Park. This course was my stomping grounds; no other race would have been as satisfying.

The marathon was an escape from the turmoil within the walls of my home. It served that second purpose to tone my body in hopes of keeping the focus and love of my husband. I was proud of the image I created, and at the same time, I pushed my cardio limits. I felt sexy again. Even my flat ass sat a little nicer after years of training. I started to get more prolonged stares and words of congratulations at my apparent changes. Leif might have even liked when other guys gave me attention. I soaked a lot of it up and tried to heal some of the deepest parts of my heart. I felt seen, desired, and like I was more than just a mother. I was ready for the acknowledgment and compliments on my weight loss and sudden fitness addiction from men and women alike. As with everything, I also didn't appreciate Leif's friends' or coworkers' lewd comments or ass grabs. Someone always had to take it a step too far and make it awkward. After ten years of marriage, I already knew that I didn't have a partner that would come to my aid to defend me. As a result, I had to stand up and protect myself with my sharp tongue or my evil glare. I wanted to be recognized for my beauty, but I never liked the blurred lines that suggested I was a blatant sexual object.

The running, races, and weight loss empowered me because it was one thing in my life I seemed able to control. There were situations in my marriage that I needed to do something about, but I just couldn't think about the effort that would take. So instead, I pushed my body to master a 26.2 race when I never considered myself a runner. I was unable to do what I needed to, so I ran.

..

It was bound to happen. People who drank and drove regularly played a numbers game. At some point, your luck ran out. On a late summer night, I awoke to a call from Leif's best friend.

"Leif got picked up for a DUI. His truck got impounded, and you can get him up at the jail in the morning. I am sorry, Heather."

After an evening of fishing, his high speeds got him pulled over. Court documents stated he was belligerent with the officer during the sobriety tests. I was so enmeshed with him and his mental health needs it blurred where he stopped and where I started. The weight of his arrest crashed down on me; my biggest concern was how Leif would react to this devastating event.

"Where would this mentally send him?"

The following day, I found a babysitter for the girls and headed to the commanding brick building. I stood in the lobby and waited behind the thick glass. The side door buzzed and out walked my husband. I didn't feel anger as he approached me. He looked bruised and fragile, and I believed the role I needed to play in that moment was crucial.

I wanted him to feel my unconditional love and support. I believed any reactions laced with judgment could send him over the edge of the cliff. I became the focused, strong wife who picked up the pieces and righted the situation. Protecting him from the gravity of the situation was the best way I could handle the reality our family faced.

This DUI created a new nugget of hope within me for his reha-bilitation. A charge like this comes with many hoops and costs. In my mind, I was already trying to stack the deck in our favor. I envisioned that promising result that I desperately wanted.

"Now! Grab the golden opportunity, Leif."

I firmly believed he would see the light and acknowledge the fallout from his choices. Then, we could get back on track with the life we had dreamed of. Rehabilitation requirements included Mothers Against Drunk Driving classes and whiskey plates placed on our vehicles (so we could be identified as high risk for intoxicated driving). Since I was also on our vehicle titles, his public badge of shame became mine. This was another price I paid for someone else's choices.

..

I don't know if Leif grasped at straws as much as I did, but I em-braced any purchase that might lead to an extra ounce of positivity in our family. One spring, we purchased a used camper. It offered more room and the ability to pull the boat simultaneously (a "gift" to lift his spirits a couple of years back). We picked up the camper the day after my 35th birthday and our 10th wedding anniversary. The excitement of a 5th wheel parked in our driveway was contagious, and we declared a family sleepover that night to test it out.

As late afternoon turned to evening, Leif made me aware of a bon-fire bachelor party at a friend's house a handful of miles away. Natural-ly, he wanted to be there.

"No! We have a sleepover with the girls in the camper tonight."

I put my foot down. Asking to leave on our wedding anniversary and break those plans with the girls was out of the question.

"You can't drive there anyway," was the logic I offered since he had already been drinking.

His requests became insistent until they were no longer a negoti-ation. He didn't require my permission to attend the bachelor party; there hadn't been a moment when he planned to stay home with his family. My panic and begging ascended to a new level.

"No, just no! You cannot drink and drive!"

"You can't let the girls down! They are already asleep in the camper."

"It's our anniversary!"

Alone, I climbed the steps into the new camper where the girls were sound asleep. I sobbed to myself as I watched his taillights leave our driveway. I felt one more bout of hope laced with panic. I made one last attempt. He received a phone call full of pleading, as I had never done before. Yet, the vehicle never slowed, and I was defeated.

I awoke to the sound of tires on the gravel driveway and lights shining in the camper windows. A car idled outside as the camper door swung open, and three silhouettes stood in the doorway. Two guys supported Leif and assisted him up the stairs. Then, just as quickly, the door closed, and the figures retreated to their vehicle. The slam of two car doors resonated before they left the driveway. He took one step, then another, before he crashed forward. The dining table was no match for the dead weight of this grown man. The cacophony of splintering wood and cracking objects rocketed through the camper. There lay my husband, crumpled in an awkward position on the floor, half under the broken table. Noise erupted from behind me as the girls reacted out of a dead sleep. Their screams were all I could hear. I think I screamed too. It didn't matter. I switched hats from the abandoned wife to the tender mother that needed to gather her babies and move them to a safer space in the house.

The following day, I tried to wake the sleeping lad for our joint birthday party lunch at my parent's house. He wasn't sober yet and couldn't stay awake. I wrote him a note, gathered the girls, and went to celebrate. I cried. I looked and felt wild. Even though the tension was palpable, there was a limited conversation about his absence from the party. We continued with what a typical party should look like, with one guest of honor missing.

..

That same night was our friends' wedding. My emotions were in overdrive, and I wasn't thinking clearly. I wanted to blow off some steam and have some beverages. I wanted retribution. I was beyond furious; I couldn't look at him and speak without hissing. The directives for the evening were as follows:

You are going to be the sober driver tonight.

I need tonight with my friends.

I don't even want to see you until it is time to go home.

I held up my side of the deal. I sat in the window seat of the regal Greysolon Ballroom as I lamented to my friends for sympathy and then promptly went downstairs to the martini bar. The beautiful, bubbly concoction smoking from the dry ice felt light and carefree, just the way I wanted it to be. Let me float. Let me be free. That night I drank, bitched, and danced. I avoided him the entire night.

A husband-friend looked at me near the end of the evening and asked, "What's wrong with Leif?"

"What do you mean? I haven't seen him all night."

Trent's explanation brought me to my knees, "He is a wreck at the bar."

My composure crumbled, and I sobbed into his shoulder. Female friends looked concerned, and Trent was caught off guard. He was a long-time friend of Leif's and a part of his group. These boys rarely passed judgment, so his questioning of the behavior was out of character. I walked onto the dance floor and let the beat of the music take over; I cried, danced, and died inside.

I tried to sober up to drive us home, but there is a specific timeline to do this effectively (I learned this from his alcohol awareness classes). So for the remainder of the night, I drank water and cried an equal amount of tears.

I drove us home in his truck with him passed out at his door. Halfway home, fate stared me right in the eyes as a car drove straight at us in the wrong lane. The earlier alcohol slowed my reflexes, and I struggled to engage. I was frozen and stared into the lights as I waited to see what would happen. The other vehicle veered off the road at the last minute, and I kept driving. I kept my eyes forward and willed the truck to the safety of our driveway.

..

Journal Entry - April 9, 2011

Anger
Anxiety
Betrayal
Queasy
Tired
Sad
Lonely
Predictable
Pain
Regretful
Beaten
Rejected
Always 2nd

..

These past two nights had me standing at the edge of sanity. Like a Tarot "Fool" card, I stood at a precipice, looking out into my unknown future. I couldn't see further than one step in front of me, but I knew something had to change significantly. Leif woke the next day and immediately started shaking, crying, and detoxing. A neighbor came to check his blood pressure, which was off the charts. My heart, so bruised from this man, looked at him and felt nothing but compassion. I loved who he used to be and believed he could be that man again. As he sat in our hand-me-down recliner, I reverted to the nurturer and pressed my body onto his to subdue his shaking.

We went together to his doctor the next day. The three of us honestly talked about Leif's consumption and its effects on his body in the limelight. The doctor prescribed anti-anxiety pills and a day treatment program, or at the very least, Alcoholics Anonymous. I felt hopeful as we left the doctor's office.

Leif talked himself out of all treatment. He didn't need any help.

Months later, he had a follow-up doctor appointment scheduled. I had seen him slip back into anger and anxiety and asked if he would request to increase the dosage of his recent medication or try a different one. My inquiry tipped his scales, and he was pissed off. How dare I suggest he wasn't well? He sped recklessly around corners and made sure I knew he was offended. Our girls sat quietly in the back seat as we drove to an anniversary dinner for my parents. After that high-tension drive, I slipped my mask into place as we entered the restaurant. The family picture taken at the celebration shows me wearing my new black pants, a flowing scarf draped over my shoulders and standing next to my family. The well-disguised mask didn't hint at the terror and anguish running through my soul.

..

Journal Entry - January 2011

Dear Fatty,

So, we meet again. Why don't you just stay away? I set these lofty goals - I even ran a MARATHON - all in the hope to keep you away. Low and behold, even while training you decided to take a peek back. You remind me of a failure. Just like the rest of America - aren't you better than that? How can you watch Fat Camp, get inspired, and eat nachos at the same time? Don't you know that your husband prefers the healthier version? All the good intentions - food choices and exercise haven't been enough to fix or hide the problem! Well, it's time for a permanent change! To actually feel PRIDE at my successes instead of excuses and hiding. No more eating unaccountability. No more panicking. No more beating yourself up - you are only human. I'm ready to always be proud. Always safe in whatever clothes. It's time for you to join forces and make some changes and commitments!

-Your Skinny Self

Hey, Skinny,

If only it were that easy! I've had a lot of emotional stress - marriage, infertility, family - and the food helped me get through. When I didn't feel like I could turn anywhere else, something sweet is always there! But, my faith is growing, my bucket is filling, no matter if the stress goes away. I'd rather not feel the shame and guilt on TOP of life's stresses. I will commit.

-Fat Bitch

..

While the storms raged, my need to control grew stronger. I needed distraction. My bruised inner child believed that hard work and good deeds brought about love, so I reverted to that system. I had played the classroom assistant role for three years at the elementary school; I needed to be a teacher again. A local Master's program as a Reading Specialist caught my attention, and I could kill two birds with one stone: earn my teacher license back and pad my resume for a more influential position. I was back in the educational saddle as I took online and in-person classes at a local college. I continued to work at the elementary school and managed the storms that raged within the walls of my home. It was anything but easy. I often found myself locked in the make-shift office of our fifth-wheel camper, where I spent hours writing papers and escaping from part of my reality.

With one year of advanced schooling under my belt, the state renewed my expired license. I applied for any local full-time English teaching position within an hour's radius of our home. The girls were out of primary school and had gained independence. I was offered one job interview, which turned into an offer. If accepted, I could be a middle and high school English teacher one hour and 15 minutes away. From a hammock, my husband and I discussed the pros and cons of my invitation. Instead of the thrill that comes with opportunity, I felt overwhelmed. I knew this would add another layer of stress to my relationship with my husband. He didn't see it this way. From his financial perspective, we hadn't been a full-time, dual-income household for almost a decade, and we agreed this new chapter should start. With the acceptance of that job, I made an invaluable choice that started me on a roadmap toward my sanity and independence.

I had a full schedule that demanded I teach many preps throughout the year, along with the assignment of a theater director. Small school districts needed bodies to fill these roles for their students. Except for the church, I had never performed in a play, let alone grasped the many facets of production. If I wanted the teaching job, I learned how to direct theater. My new plate of responsibilities was what I needed. I connected with humans outside my zip code and left behind the stress of home life for hours each day. I controlled this part of my life.

This new position and time commitment were a blessing, and a curse all rolled into one. Leif's monsters yelled even louder when I was out of sight. He didn't have access to these parts of me: my work email account, relationship with coworkers and students, or my new sense of purpose. His frustrations intensified and the accusations got louder.

Oh, how I loved being back in front of the class. I put on a different mask to connect with the students and teach quality content: forced confidence. Being ridiculous and loving for my students shined a small light inside me when I needed it most. I embraced the community, leadership opportunities, and families. When I walked into those school doors, I relaxed as I inhaled a scent that resembled safety and acceptance.

The pulse of our home was throbbing and tense; my nerves were taut and frazzled. Any joyful moments experienced in our household over the course of these last three years were superficial, with an undercurrent of toxic energy always at play. Finally, I wrote an email to one of my closest friends and admitted how completely broken I was. I had separated from my friends over the past few years and felt I should explain. I confessed the severity of Leif's drinking and suggested that mental health issues might also be at play. I voiced and gave life to my fears and was terrified.

We motored across Minnesota to spend an extended weekend at our favorite resort. This family time was typically a reset with a healthy dose of relaxation, cable TV, and swimming. However, in the middle of the night, blinding lights flooded the bedroom, and I woke from a sound sleep. This man, my husband, screamed over me in bed. It happened so suddenly that I struggled to orient myself. I couldn't translate the accusations that came my way as he followed me around the bedroom and into the living room.

"Slow down. I can't understand you," I said. "Leif, don't wake the girls."

He couldn't hear me, and his rage was palpable. While I slept and he drank, he dug through the different folders of our joint email account (this was the only type of email account he allowed). He found and read my email to Trish in the "sent" file. I paid the price. He screamed and paced in agitation; he wanted to wake the girls and leave. He despised me and wanted to bolt. I convinced him that we didn't need to go that minute. Thankfully, no noise or movement came from the direction of the girls' bedroom. He retreated into our bedroom and shut the door. I felt his anger lingering in the space he left, pulsing, pushing, and strangling.

I made it to the plaid couch, where I lay down in the fetal tuck and faced inward. I sank into a semi-awake coma, feeling petrified and numb. My head was void of thoughts or rational emotions. A praise song from church looped in my mind like a mantra. I don't know if it was the words that comforted me or the connection to my higher power reminding me that I wasn't alone. I clung to those protective words wondering if the music faded off, would I fade off too?

Come, now is the time to worship
Come, now is the time to give your heart
Come, just as you are to worship
Come, just as you are before your God
Come
We finished out the vacation, but I don't have a single memory

after that night, whether we stayed for one night more or five. I do remember that once we arrived home, I went into the bedroom, stood by the corner window, and made a phone call to one of my best friends and recipient of that email.

"I am sorry. I shouldn't have sent that email to you, Trish. Everything is okay."

The phone call was awkward, and she didn't know what to say. So I quickly ended our connection. I returned to the living room and tried to earn back a shred of forgiveness from my husband.

..

Paulo Coelho's famous work, *The Alchemist*, suggests, "And when you want something, all the universe conspires in helping you to achieve it." Unfortunately, I didn't feel like the universe was conspiring in my favor, nor had it given me any graces to find my way out of this perpetual hell. I was far down a hole and couldn't see the light.

Smarter people whisper, "Why doesn't she just walk out that door and stand up for herself?"

"People accept the love they think they deserve," and I was a prime example. If Leif had been physically abusive, I can't say with 100% certainty that I would've packed up and left. I loved him. I had hope and believed in the vows we had shared. I trusted that people had the power to change.

Later in our marriage, I recognized that I had this man on a pedestal. Emotional abuse is sneaky. I allowed him to control me through guilt, shame and gaslighting, just like my mother did. I was codependent. Accepting their accusations and believing I needed to act better was easy for me.

As the emotional abuse intensified, my survival ability as a mother required him to be at work, at a lake, or off in the woods. The only other time his rage became silent was when he passed out at night. I purchased a book about being in a toxic, emotionally abusive relationship from Amazon. It came with a disguised title and cover, specifically to protect its reader from the suspicion of their abuser. I drank in the words and advice into my parched soul, yet ironically, I was no closer to taking action. I still hoped he'd forgive my transgressions and life could settle down. A part of me still believed I was to blame for his unhappiness and that I might be able to fix it. I wasn't on a path to leave him yet

..

Journal Entry - November, 2011

Dear Skinny Girl,

I realize you are not far away. I'm sorry that I keep making choices that push you away. But I am realizing who I am and what being skinny and healthy means. I am ready for that physical change - and spiritual change. I am coming back - I'm going to shed this layer. And when I get there, I am going to be more radiant than before. God's love will make me strong, appropriate, and happy! I don't need to fear inappropriate situations. Be patient.

- Girl with the Baggy Sweater On

Dear Hoodie Girl,

I knew you wanted to come back. You are going to want to shed those hoodies at some point and get out of the darkness. I believe you can and I'll be waiting. Keep your sites forward and trust in God.

-That Girl That Ran a Marathon

Before 2018

"One of the hardest things you'll ever have to do, my dear,
is to grieve the loss of a person who is still alive."

— Jeannette Walls, *The Glass Castle*

..

May of 2012 was a month of celebration, joy, and tragedy all wrapped together. I concluded my first year manning a classroom and directed two successful plays. Our best friends had their first baby after many years of infertility. Leif and I motored down to their city to welcome this joy. My eyes welled with tears as I watched my best friend, Liz, hold her baby girl. Joe fell ill the previous days, and we joked about his resistance to his new role as a dad.

Nine days later, when most moms relished the first days with their infant, this momma called me, crying, "Joe left me. He took the dog and went to the cabin. Heather, he left me."

My first thought was, "Is it April Fool's Day?"

It couldn't be; it was the end of May. These two were high school sweethearts and had battled infertility for years. A new baby girl had just entered the picture! Their relationship in turmoil was unthinkable.

"He must be panicking."

I ran right toward the discomfort and heavy emotions. I had no other option; my person needed me. So her older sister and I kept the walls standing that weekend. Between phone calls to triage this disaster, her sister and I met the baby's needs, and we also held the new momma's mental health as she grieved. Her sister, Leif, and I stood in the messy middle, communicating to figure out what was happening. Leif and I were the glue - what an irony.

Joe never came home and ended his relationship and marriage with Liz. He abandoned her with a newborn baby and left her with many broken dreams. This was a tough weekend for me. I wasn't an emotional rock myself, but I gave her all I had because she needed what she deserved.

Leif and I returned home from our respective locations and embraced immediately. There was no tension between us, no evidence of discord.

While we embraced, I said, "We can never let that happen to us."

Two days later, he didn't come home after fishing with friends

for the day. The girls came home from school to an empty house. I
punched the numbers into the phone with alarm and tried to reach
him. He took a multi-hour detour to the strip club and bar. He answered the phone with music playing loudly in the background, laced
with the voices of the barflies. He promised to come right home; he
continued to drink for hours. Finally, on his schedule, he drove home. I
watched the headlights on his Ford Ranger illuminate the darkness as
he drove down the driveway toward our house.

My resolution shifted as I lit a match and threw it on the last bridge
holding together our marriage. It went up in flames. This straw broke
the camel's back, even though it wasn't the most painful of events we
had experienced. I think I broke at that moment, after offering so much
emotional energy to Liz the past weekend and this whole marriage for
years. I could not take one step forward carrying my parcel of hope. I
was done.

The next day I looked at the man I had vowed to love until death
did us part and knew I had to leave him. I finally believed that I deserved better; our girls deserved better. I wanted to breathe again. I
could offer the girls stability 50% of the time, which was better than
100% of the time with this trauma. I waited for someone to drop me
a lifeline, but that time was up. I no longer wanted to wait for him to
decide he wanted something better for himself, our marriage, or our
family. I was done.

..

Once I decided to leave this toxic dumpster fire relationship, I never
reconsidered. Done meant done. I walked taller and felt bulletproof. I
naively ignored the extensive mourning I needed to do. Healing wasn't
my focus when my concern was survival and stability. The people I lost,
the finances I lacked, and the home I needed to recreate overwhelmed
me. Support from my parents wasn't happening. My divorce seemed
too difficult for them, making my head and heart more of a mess. These
losses didn't stop me from walking away from the only life I had known.
That same life had destroyed me for years, and I wanted out.

..

In the movies, many divorcing parents are staged gathering the family share of the upcoming changes. A semi-healthy dialogue shows two supporting parents explaining to the children how much they are loved, even if Mommy and Daddy cannot remain together. I am sure there are families that attempt a sense of normalcy like this. For the families without enough balance, the responsibility falls on one of the parents. Near the end of May of 2012, I sat my girls down to deliver that exact message. Tears stung the back of my eyes before I began to speak.

"Girls, there are going to be some changes to our family," I began.

Their innocent eyes looked down at me as I sat on the floor. I was so broken, I could never have sat above them for this conversation.

"Your dad isn't super healthy right now. We are getting a divorce," I said.

Tears started flowing from all three of us; although I am not sure which of us added a whimpering sound.

"I love you so, so much. I will do the best I can to support you. I know it will be hard." I barely squeaked out. "I am so sorry."

We held each other and let the raw emotions emerge. They may have been young girls, but they understood how difficult the situation was and that life wouldn't ever be the same.

..

I hadn't known how to stand up and fight for myself. I wanted someone to take my hand and help me make the super hard decisions. I viewed it from a victim's standpoint for so much of my life. What didn't go as I had planned? Who had wronged me? Where could I place the blame for how I felt? Yes, bad shit happens. But, I couldn't see that I had to change my identity if I wanted different results. I left, which was monumental, but the celebration didn't last long.

My biggest hurdle was finding somewhere to land as I put the pieces of my life back in place. After an emotional round table discussion, my dad offered a safe dwelling for our transition period. He invited me to move in with the girls until I could get back on my feet. As I drove away, feeling like the stress had been relieved, he called and rescinded the offer. I desperately needed this help and was blindsided by their change of heart. I took it personally; I couldn't understand and felt cut off at the knees.

Mother called on my drive to work the following day and clarified that my dad's offer hadn't sat well with her. She didn't want to feel uncomfortable around Leif. She wanted her role as grandma clear without the mixed messages of her as the girls' caretaker. As that door from my parents slammed shut in my face, a new one appeared and remained open. Kathy was a friend's mother and knew my story. She had been married to an alcoholic for decades. This angel offered me a sanctuary, rent-free until I saw a plan for my fresh start.

..

The separation was hard. We debated bills and money, and Lief limited my access to our finances for almost a year. Meaningful relationships fell apart: in-laws, friends, and people who picked sides. Lawyers assisted in dividing fourteen years "equally." He fought dirty in the settlement, and I walked away from equity and money. I was tired and had no fight left in me. I needed a more assertive lawyer who advised and advocated for me when I couldn't. I craved someone to lead my life because I couldn't seem to function alone.

It was a pivotal point in my life when I knew I deserved better and left my husband. I couldn't understand why life was still so heavy and difficult. I was a warrior badass who had done what I was supposed to. Even though I left the trauma behind, I continued to carry all the leftover emotions and hurts no matter how far forward I walked. My stand to prevent future abuse was a huge step in the right direction, but processing feelings and healing scars take more than a new address. Plain and simple, I didn't know how to heal.

..

Over the many years, including after our divorce, my friendship with Liz had been steady. We never got into petty arguments or held terrible feelings. She saw all the angles of my marriage dynamic and the uptick in Leif's alcoholism. She loved both of us - me and Leif. I could be vulnerable with her and share many of the darkest moments. Liz was my lifeline; she was the person I turned to for compassion and understanding.

Two different truths came my way from my soul sister during the final years of my marriage. She believed Lief loved me no matter how he treated me and tended to excuse his behavior because of this fact. At the same time, she also thought he was going to make me leave him. His actions were not improving, the results were worsening, and my life was crumbling - and she saw it all. She planted that seed long before it resonated inside of me. I heard her words, but I couldn't process them. She was right.

Joe left Liz less than one week before I announced I had given up on my marriage. Our lives felt woven together even as they tore apart. Liz and I spoke every day for months as we drowned in life's circumstances. We tossed a life preserver back and forth to each other, barely able to catch our breath before we needed to offer it back.

Our scenarios were different, but the rawness of trauma resonated for us both. Liz had been knocked off her feet, blindsided by abandonment. I was broken from years of abuse. My mind and body were a shell of who I had been. I didn't have much of a support system in place. My emotions were too high with my parents, and I resisted being around them. I needed Liz.

..

Once I opened my heart and allowed my fears to have an authentic voice, I became overwhelmed. The mask I wore had kept the terror under wraps, but now I couldn't ignore it. So I turned up the volume on my truth and inner voice, and it told me, "Do something!" I sought help from a women's shelter. I diligently answered their questionnaire about the situations in my life and they quickly validated the extreme level of toxicity. They were concerned physical violence was inevitable and advised me to request authorities present when gathering my

belongings. Through the fog I heard them and appreciated the validation, but didn't take their advice.

I moved into Kathy's borrowed space. I wasn't allowed back into
the home I had built with Leif to sort or pack. He graciously packed
for me and placed treasures with garbage in unlabeled boxes. He froze
our finances, and that significantly limited my options. I couldn't block
out his anger and resentment; it was still everywhere. The move had
not cut the cords with my abuser. He still had control of my life. I felt
paralyzed and alone.

I learned how to breathe again during the six weeks at Kathy's
townhome. Coparenting with Leif was stressful. My main priority
was to find stable housing for the girls and myself before the school
year started in the fall. Mid-summer, I loaded up my meager possessions from Kathy's townhome and moved us into my aunt's camper.
The space was small and temporary, but it worked. Unfortunately, the
days ticked by, and I needed a more permanent solution. This camper
wouldn't work for our schools or the Minnesota winter. I was so tired.

..

During the summer of 2012, Duluth's housing market was stable.
Home prices were fair, and buyers had time to consider purchasing.
My standards were low, and I looked for any home with a sound roof
and walls. My spirit guides led me to a cozy bungalow, and I signed a
contract to purchase it. Since Leif refused to release our finances until the divorce settlement, I figured out there was no way I could buy
that home. It felt like a tremendous setback. I never considered renting
a more manageable path; I was hyper-focused on buying. Finally, I
pivoted and asked if the seller would consider a contract for the deed.
The seller agreed to the new terms as long as I gave her a healthy down
payment.

Even securing the down payment was a battle. I assumed our divorce would have progressed and money would be made available.
That didn't happen. I pleaded for funds for the benefit of our daughters, but it fell on deaf ears. Finally, when it appeared that I couldn't

purchase this home, Aunt Julie offered to lend me the money for the down payment. The HUD settlement came the night before closing. I gasped at the total I needed to bring to the closing table the next day. It was $1,400. I didn't have enough money. Matters worsened when Julie's down payment check didn't show up in the mail on time. As my aunt motored up the shore to my Grandma and Grandpa's house, I cast a bigger safety net.

"Would you lend us the money until my check arrives? Heather needs help," she asked her parents.

Grandma went to their safe, withdrew over 20k in cash, and handed it over. Just the right people helped me provide a safe space for my daughters, and I took none of it for granted.

..

The big girls were overwhelmed by the heavy emotional load of the separation. After I moved out, the girls went on a week-long camping trip out West with my parents. They returned drowning in emotional baggage. Not yet preteens, they were subjected to family strife without a filter from my parents. I was so excited to see them, but I saw the turmoil on their faces in my rearview mirror. Their hearts were young and vulnerable and deserved a vacation full of ice cream cones and amusement parks, but that wasn't what they received. Instead, their vacation kept them fully engulfed in the emotions of a messy divorce between their parents, seen through the eyes of their grieving grandparents.

The three-day custody rotation was in effect soon after our separation. This rotation accommodated Leif's work schedule and proved the most straightforward answer. I felt so much fear and anxiety when they were with their dad; I didn't trust him to make healthy decisions while being the sole parent. Sure enough, Leila returned from her dad's an emotional mess.

"Dad drove us home, and it was so late. He had been drinking at the fire with friends. I was so scared."

I called Child Protective Services each time the girls reported this story to me, and there was nothing they could do.

They advised me, "Something needs to happen for us to intervene. Or someone else needs to call as it is happening."

This was the system and its boundaries. They believed I might be a bitter ex-wife retaliating or providing false information. It is a failed system that advises a mother who tries to protect her children from harm to wait until an injury happens. I couldn't understand how they treated the situation as if the tears and fear my children experienced were not harmful enough; let's just wait for something more significant.

I offered my children a safe word they could use with one of the other moms at the party, "purple penguins." They could also try to call me, but he was unlikely to allow that. So they needed to find help and stay out of his car.

I offered their father a threat in-person (that I tape-recorded). I told him about the girls' confessions and fears.

"Do you think I believe you were drinking Mountain Dew at 2 AM at the Olson's house? If you drink and drive with the girls again, the wrath I will bring down on you will be like nothing you have experienced from me."

I had more fights in me when faced with protecting my cubs. The girls never again came to me distraught over drinking and driving with their dad.

..

I was so proud of my accomplishments as a runner. This non-athlete girl ran races! I fantasized about getting a tattoo that would highlight my achievements. I asked a couple of graphic artist friends if they wanted to help me design something meaningful, and I hoped their creativity would bring the design to life. Finding the courage to voice this desire felt a little un-Heatherlike. Unfortunately, neither graphic designer took the bait I dangled, so the tattoo remained a loose dream in the back of my mind.

I had a more significant feat worth branding on my skin. I did the unimaginable and stepped away from my abusive marriage. Again,

I wanted to mark myself and commemorate the warrior strength I displayed. This time, the inspirational design came into focus quickly without needing validation from anyone. I found myself at Anchor's End Tattoo parlor, where I got my first tattoo. I went from Baptist rule follower to tattooed badass overnight.

The design landed on the inside of my right wrist. A tree branch swept into a circle, ending with a cross at its root; the word "courage" inked the circle space. I craved the pain from the needle as it marked a badge of my journey. This was the first of many trauma therapy tattoos I placed on my body.

My first tattoo shined at me, "I am a survivor."

I posted on Facebook and said it was the best $100 I had ever spent because it was. But, unfortunately, this post didn't go over well with my parents. This simple tattoo, less than four inches long, widened the divide that had already pulled us apart. The joy I felt over my sovereignty was clouded when my dad accused me of being on drugs.

"Everyone is praying for you."

In their eyes, evil was devouring me, the lost sheep. Their prayers suggested I needed help and saving. The irony is that I had needed help and saving for the previous four years. So, where was that call to action when I needed it?

..

As the first Christmas separated came into view, I was unstable at best. My mental health, financial bearings, and relationship with my parents scraped rock bottom, but knowing that letter was waiting if I needed it gave me the courage to finish the school year. Their negative reaction to my tattoo had left me feeling even more damaged and separate from who they wanted me to be. I chose not to attend the family holiday; Leif attended with the girls as their guest of honor. I spent Christmas Eve with my girls and dropped them off after dinner. Intense dread filled my chest as I entered the cold, dark bungalow that would be my "party" for the rest of the holiday. I was distraught with loneliness. I left Christmas morning and just drove. With no destina-

tion in mind, I landed in Madison, Wisconsin, and spent the holiday in
a sparse hotel room. Christmas in Madison was just as devastating as
it would have been back in Duluth. I tried to outrun my bone-crushing
emotions, but they followed me like a shadow.

..

Wells was the guy behind the coffee bar with a curly head of hair
and a full beard. He wasn't a big man, and his mannerisms were unique.
His quirkiness intrigued me. I'd been separated for seven months and
had only dabbled with light dating. Wells was awkward and creative
and unlike my former husband. So I set my sights and forced my way in
with the conversation, mild flirting, and social media connections. Our
friendship landed itself on the first date on Valentine's Day 2013. We
went to Buffalo Wild Wings, and I wrote him a Valentine's limerick.

His apartment was simple, yet it included a bougie espresso mak-
er and an excessive collection of candles, and bubble bath. Wells was
ideal in my eyes: his faith was strong, and he served at our church.
He hadn't been married or had any children and a limited amount of
family and friends. In my mind, this meant "no baggage." He grew up
in Oklahoma and went to a private religious school that gave swats to
misbehaving students as punishment, even into the 1990s. His past was
pretty void of girlfriends. I didn't see this as peculiar since religion was
his moral compass. His naivety and innocence around intimacy were
a challenge for me.

"No, I don't think you need to wear jeans to bed if you ever spend
the night. We can control ourselves."

My new chapter with a boyfriend started as I spread my wings.
Finally, I truly believed I was ready for a relationship.

..

The discord and conflict between me, my parents, and my sister
were palpable. Wells and I had dated for a month when I received
an unexpected email from Mother. I opened it and found a link to a
recorded sermon about honoring your parents. I felt guilt and a tinge
of resentment. My bubbling emotions spilled over as I listened to the

speech. It was dense with Bible verses and expectations. I told Wells about the delivered message and that I needed to talk to my parents.

I called in sick to school before I texted my mom, "We need to talk." I suggested she call dad home from work to be there, and I invited Ann to join too. My emotions ran from spite to hope, looped back to hunger. I needed my parents now more than I ever had. Wells said he would go and support me; I wouldn't walk into the lion's den alone.

I walked into the back porch with this odd man at my arm and met an emotional wall that had me pause. My parents and Ann stood on the upper landing and looked down at us with red, swollen eyes. I sensed he made them uncomfortable as a stranger in their home but invited us to sit in the living room. The arrangement felt formal, just like the family meetings from a decade ago. Shock waves of guilt and shame lapped over me as I waited for someone to say something.

Mother said, "We do not feel honored by you as your parents."

I countered, "My time with Leif was so horrible. The alcoholism. His extreme emotional and sexual abuse that I endured. I was drowning."

"We didn't know."

My body felt tense before my heart understood they were not receiving my messages.

Frustration and fear started taking over the conversation, "I didn't have time to send the memo. But, mother, you cried when I told you I was leaving him. You said you had been scared the past year and worried he was too rough with the girls. You knew something wasn't right."

I continued, "The fact that you still associate with him. . .that he was invited to your Christmas is fucked up."

That one f-bomb was the ammunition they needed to take the upper hand. Their accusations increased, and my footing faltered.

"You disrespected us when you had people in our house nine months ago. You hosted a party and put a scratch on the table! If you want to see the booze bottle, it is downstairs!"

The one time Wells spoke up, "You have a booze bottle in the basement from nine months ago? Why?"

Nine months before, I stayed at my childhood home and tried to find sanity and safety enough to create a plan to leave Leif. When I hosted this party, my parents had been on vacation with our girls. I had invited a handful of close friends to be with me, and it was one of the more supportive moments of my life. These women let me cry, lent a hand, and gave me a financial gift that helped me take the first steps toward freedom. But instead, my parents defaced something key to my survival; they stripped it of joy.

I made one last attempt, "You haven't been supporting the girls. They need you. They deserve extra love and support right now."

My dad's words brought our conversation to a close, "We are scared to call you. But now we know we can call, and we will! As far as you, I cannot care anymore. I gave it to GOD!"

His tone was emotional and agitated, and his final words cut the most, "You have changed. We wish you were on drugs so we could fix you."

This wasn't the first or last time I had heard they were scared of me. Who had I become, or what had I done, to make them feel scared? I had spent the past four years frozen in my own trauma and was finally finding my footing to something healthier. Did that scare them? I stood up and left. It had been a long 15 minutes.

..

Well's minimalistic lifestyle and limited relational experiences quickly went from cute to aggravating. He disliked children and lived a rigid, formula-dense life that needed to run right on course. A small wrench thrown into his schedule brought about a different side of him that wasn't very pleasant. The few times I brought him to events with me, he didn't fit by my side, like a square peg in a round hole. For example, I invited him to accompany me as a chaperone at my school's prom. I expected the evening to be fun and romantic, but he sat in the corner on his phone and drew curious stares. After the dance, I knew Wells was not the person I needed in my life. I called off our relationship. He struggled to understand why I was running, but I turned my back and walked away.

I refocused on teaching and wrapping up the school year. As April turned to May, I started to feel "off."

A coworker asked if I could be pregnant, and I replied, "I can't."

I hadn't kept track of my cycles nor used birth control for years. My expired relationship with Wells had been minimal on the intimacy front anyway. Still, her innocent question found an uncomfortable home in my mind. I was a past-prime single, supposedly-sterile mom nagged by the festering possibility of pregnancy, so I picked up a test. The iconic little white stick I had peed on for years reappeared. Home alone, I peed with as much grace and precision as possible. In my former life, I prayed for two little pink lines numerous times; today, I held my breath and waited. Two little pink lines innocently stared up at me from this pregnancy test. I sat down and cried.

I was pregnant.

Thoughts tried to form but got pushed out of the way by the next onslaught of inner chatter.

"How could...?"

"But we hardly...."

"What in the hell will...?"

"I have to tell...."

"Should I be happy...?"

I had no answers. I shared the news with my friend, Caryn, and she swallowed me up in a massive hug with nothing but joy. That white stick confirmed this pregnancy. I needed to tell Wells and knew this would be complex information for him. I tried to connect with him, but he wouldn't take my phone calls. I tried a different approach and reached out via text. He responded with guarded disinterest and one-word answers, but I pressed for a few minutes of his time. He refused and wanted nothing to do with the woman that had broken his heart weeks before.

I did what all panicking pregnant women do at that moment and let him have it, "You are going to be a father. I am at an event for the girls but will be in touch with you in two hours."

We met, hugged, and cried. We got back together because that made religious and practical sense. Four days later, I reached my breaking point with Wells and walked away one more time. We would need to work separately as parents because our partnership was all wrong.

The next nine months were a lot of ad-libbing. I needed to find out my lines, which scene I was acting in, or if I was the protagonist or the antagonist of my own story. They say the villain is the hero of her own story. Some friends couldn't fully mask their shock at my pregnancy announcement. I felt the waves of their pity. However, others were immediately supportive and helped me along the journey. I had not healed from my past traumas but needed to focus on my pregnancy and make it a top priority.

Wells and I only met a few times while I was pregnant. The situation was uncomfortable for both of us, so we kept our distance. We met at a coffee shop at the beginning of my 3rd trimester, setting the tone for co-parenting. He shared his well-thought-out plans to move into my neighborhood to ease shared custody. His intentions sounded sincere, yet I felt claustrophobic. He suggested every other week custody immediately after the baby was born, and my hand made complete contact with the panic button inside my chest.

I stared at him incredulously, "A baby cannot be away from its mother!"

The power of my fear far outweighed logic. I panicked and saw a looming battle over the raising of another child. All the emotions I had experienced and held onto for the past five years exploded within my body. The fear, loss, and doom felt precisely the same, even if the situation had changed. I grasped to feel in control, but everything slipped through my fingers.

I sat on the knowledge that he wanted immediate shared custody of the baby for the remainder of my pregnancy. The uncontrollable unknown had me back in a state of full panic. I felt so alone. I searched for direction and knew my two girls needed me to set a foundation for this new life, and I needed to do it NOW! My circle of friends supported me the best they could, but they had jobs and families and weren't here to save me. I leaned heavily into my Aunt Julie and Grandma to keep me looking forward. They believed in me, and that was enough to carry me.

..

The girls and I wrote a list of baby names on the fridge door with expo markers. Our favorite girls' and boys' names were on the door as we vied for selection. As the months changed, so did the words on the fridge door. Finally, I decided on the name only a few weeks before the baby's arrival. I kept the girls guessing and only told them the girl's name started with a "C" and the boy's name a "G."

As the baby's due date crept closer, Grandma sent her love and support. She made it clear that nothing would keep her from embracing her great-grandbaby, even at the age of 83.

"Heather, I will be waiting for the phone to ring!" she told me.

"I know Gram, I will call."

She said in all seriousness, "I will take a bobsled if I need to, to get to that baby!"

On the morning of delivery, I put the girls on the school bus with my clothes under my bathrobe. A baby would be born today, and our world would change. Caryn brought me to the hospital and stayed by my side, even in the delivery room. I felt the divine feminine energy in this room full of women as I welcomed my third daughter into the world. Our bare skin touched under my hospital gown as I basked in the unique beauty of those first few hours. Michelle and Leila burst into the room to read the baby bassinet with the letter "C" at the top. I named this little blessing Camille.

The strong, eccentric Heather was very present in that sunny hospital room. Right after surgery, I wore pearls like Audrey Hepburn while wrapped in my red bathrobe. I maintained that confidence the first days after birthing Camille. I firmly affixed that mask, wore the pearls, and joked with the staff; I faked it.

My mind wanted me to think, "This isn't so bad! You can be a single momma with a newborn. Way to be strong!"

The opponent, my anxiety, made an abrupt entrance 48 hours post-delivery and demanded to take center stage. It walked over to me, swiftly removed my pearl necklace, and replaced it with a tight choke-hold.

"You aren't ready for this. Heather, you failed again. Your life is a dumpster fire. You are a disappointment."

Wells came to meet his daughter. He held her and took pictures while I sat on my hospital bed. I watched with trepidation as I recalled his suggestion for immediate rotating custody. We didn't discuss custody arrangements, but he requested to bring a group of coworkers to the hospital with him the next day.

"Hell, no. I am recovering and not interested in greeting strangers in my hospital room," was my answer.

He made it to the hospital once. After that, he traveled across the state and purchased a more reliable vehicle to transport the baby.

He refused to sign the birth paperwork for unmarried parents, "I cannot be 100% sure of her parentage."

He wanted physical proof she was his child before his name appeared on her birth certificate. My skin crawled, and my mind raced as her dad had one foot in her world and one foot out. I sat in my hospital room and cried. My OB sat by my bedside, clutched my hand, and took the time to be present. She advised me to restart my anti-anxiety meds and approved my request to leave the hospital a day early. I needed to be inside the safe walls of my own home and away from this hospital.

..

The relationship with my parents was undefined and tense. Hurt feelings simmered and silence ruled. After "Heather's Intervention Party," the gap widened tenfold, and we didn't fake a shallow relationship. Now with Camille in the picture, our issues didn't seem so insurmountable to me. The family had a beautiful new life, and I wanted them to be a part of it. I still craved support and acceptance from my parents and hoped the joy of a baby would repair parts of our relationship.

I drove up the North Shore to visit with my grandma and extended family shortly after Camille's birth. I needed their love. In Grandma's eyes, she was one of her beautiful great-grandbabies, and the details didn't matter. She met my third daughter before my parents, and that bothered her. The impasse with my parents came up in conversation, and she didn't hesitate to let her tears fall. Our family matriarch preferred unity and peace (rose-colored glasses) and wanted my family to put our differences behind us. She lay it on my shoulders as her dying wish. I cried with her and let my inner child release my deep hurt. The adult Heather stayed stubborn and had no intention of being the bigger person with my parents.

Grandma wanted to have this conversation with me again on Camille's first visit to her house. She knew a year had passed since I last spoke to my parents.

Gram pushed, "It isn't right that they haven't met Camille. You need to do something about this."

Guilt and need fueled my impulsive decision to stop at my parents on the drive home that day. I wanted them to meet my daughter and see how hard I tried to be a good mother and human being who wasn't on drugs. I arrived at their doorstep unannounced. My parents opened the door as I carried the car seat with their newest granddaughter toward them. The hardship and bad feelings got placed on a back burner for the time being as they welcomed us into their home. Both parents held the pink blessing, and tears masked other emotions in the room.

We all wanted the war to end over the upcoming months. But, unfortunately, nobody called a truce, and we swept the disagreements under the rug. We tried to discuss our differences several times, but fiery emotions held a strong wall of resistance. We all wore masks to disguise our truth and pain.

..

The last time I was a new momma, I had the support of my husband and the baby's father. My journey looked and felt a little different after the birth of Camille. Wells wanted to do the right things. He called to check in on her the first two weeks before we started discussing a visiting schedule. I set my own needs aside (again) and drove her for 20 minutes to have an hour-long visit at his house. He didn't have a car seat, nor did he have much furniture. While he held his new baby girl, I sat uncomfortably on the ceramic tile floor, pretending everything was okay. My body was still healing post-surgery, and being in Wells' presence made me uncomfortable. This was our rhythm for over a month until he thought he was ready for an hour or two of unsupervised visits. I would drop her off and head to the nearby mall to pass the time.

Camille wasn't comfortable with him. He had an unmanicured beard and awkwardness in his interactions. She often cried and fussed with him, which intensified everyone's discomfort. It took around three months before I started to think more clearly and realized I didn't want to make all the effort.

"It's time for you to invest in a car seat. I will drive her one way for your visits, but you need to take care of the other," I said.

He met my request with many excuses: he didn't have enough money to buy a car seat, his vehicle was unreliable, and reminders that he had the right to see his child.

"I am not stopping you from seeing her. This is what parents do - we figure it out," I answered. "Ask your dad to drive you. Work more hours. Do what you must, but I am no longer willing to put in all the effort."

Tension started building between the two of us. However, I wasn't heartbroken when Wells canceled his Saturday morning custody visit.

"It gets too busy in the afternoon at the laundromat. Dad and I need to go this morning."

We also needed to determine paternity since he wouldn't sign the paperwork at the hospital before we left. Camille was left without health insurance since he was yet to accept responsibility. He also didn't have a child support payment obligation until his parentage was official. Looking back, I wish someone had advised me to consider the pros and cons of having him listed as her father. He was obviously resisting, but more than that, he made my life very difficult and anxious. After a terse phone conversation about health insurance, he slammed the nail into the coffin when he ended the phone call, "Good Night, Shirley."

He knew that calling me by Mother's name was about as low as he could go - and he went there. More out of spite, I took Camille to the County buildings for DNA sampling to be compared with his. Congrats, she's yours!

We had jumped through all of these hoops to establish him as the father, yet his visits became less frequent. He arrived for his first-ever pickup, having the car seat installed incorrectly. Rather than take the time with me to adjust it safely, he bolted to go home and "rig something up" to secure the car seat's placement. I didn't fight his need to run. He never did get that car seat in place. Wells took Camille on a stroller walk in early Spring when she was about four months old. That was the last time he asked to see her. I heard from him again two months later, but after that, he was never a part of her life by his own choice.

..

My friend Cyndee loved vintage campers. She refinished Little Miss Sunshine, a 1963 Shasta Compact, back to glory as a she-shed on wheels. I had forever been a fan of miniatures, and the idea of dolling up a mini camper sounded so fun. She helped me find a rare gem - a 1962 12' Fireball. The previous owners painted it a hideous red, white, and blue striped pattern outside for a country fest. However, the jewel was impeccable inside. Most of its original interior was intact and in pristine condition. It housed a turquoise gas oven, a mid-century dinette, and the original woodwork. I purchased this camper for a couple of hundred dollars with my heart set on creating a space for new family memories.

The girls and I focused on that little camper and healed inside and outside while we encouraged our creative juices to flow. We sanded down the 3-toned exterior and painted it back to the original Fireball markings. I sewed feminine pastel panels for curtains, painted the interior walls white, and made sunny cushion covers. The dinette wasn't practical for sleep, so I remodeled it into a permanent double bed. We even set down new vinyl tiles on the floor after we scraped the shag carpet and its decades-old residue. We invested in a hopeful future as we returned this little camper to her previous glory. The most popular girl's name in 1962 was Lisa, so Miss Lisa was born.

For our only trip as a family of four girls, we trekked across Minnesota in search of the three Paul Bunyan landmarks. I towed that camper behind my minivan (named Effie) and backed it into a State Park campsite like a pro. We ventured out and met the first Paul Bunyan at a family park. It spoke the girls' names as we entered as if it had expected us to visit. The park was entertaining, but we seemed to force the feeling of fun and normalcy. Two summers ago, we were a complete family and camped regularly. Last summer, we were homeless, and I tried to find a new way of life for us. We had grown into a family of four, and we all tried to find comfort and contentment with everything new. Unfortunately, we weren't there yet.

We experienced a ridiculous amount of mosquitoes who weren't happy about our shared riverside campsite. The fairy tale abruptly halted as the sun set on our first night. The pests swarmed, and the big girls couldn't sleep in the back of the minivan. Baby Camille and I slept on the shared bed while Michelle and Leila crunched tight on the floor in sleeping bags. The bugs buzzed, the baby fussed, and I fretted. We never made it to the other Bunyan landmarks; we packed camp the following day and headed home.

Miss Lisa remained in our lives for four more years, sometimes used for camping and others as an eccentric lawn decoration. But then, I was forced to sell her when my financial needs took center stage.

Thankfully the couple that purchased Miss Lisa had great energy and planned to appreciate her.

..

That fall, one of my cousins lost his life. He was talented and funny and left the Earth far too soon. Our whole family felt immense loss. At the funeral, I sat away from the family with my nine-month-old baby. Communication had somehow reverted to uncomfortable silence with my parents. Forced pleasantries weren't available at a funeral, so I sat alone with Camille.

My emotions were stretched to the maximum as I managed a baby and my grief during the funeral. Being "separate" from the family added to the tension. I got through that day but vowed never to ever subject myself to that stress level again.

I promised, "I will never walk into a funeral alone again. I will hire a man to be by my side for support if I need to."

..

Dating as a single mom looked different from the earlier years of high school and college. I picked my high school sweetheart out of a team of basketball players based on the opinion that he had the best armpit hair. That started a solid, four-year relationship. Those rules didn't apply now. The men I met had experienced life and carried their baggage. Online dating was ridiculous and laced with many unsolicited dick pics. One gentleman told me he was a vampire. Another suitor went to court for missed child support; he didn't have enough to support himself, his parents, and his kids. The parts of my unhealed self sprinted in the other direction as soon as a detail felt wrong. My spidey sense turned me rigid and fearful.

"I have baggage. Do you have baggage? Let's compare our past relationships and see if our damage can blend into something new and amazing," was adult dating.

Joey was different from the recent string of online matches. I dubbed him "Superman" early on and placed him on a superhuman pedestal. He walked with an air of confidence and made no apologies for the circumstances of his life. He wore a "don't mess with me" edge that made me feel safe. Finally, I had the resident badass in my corner.

"Look at me, Mom, Dad, and Leif, I have this badass shield right next to me, and HE is going to get my life back on track! So you can't mess with me anymore!"

His life was transitioning, so he accepted the stable basics I offered him: home, car, and ambition. But, unfortunately, my needy self clung right back to him. We dated for a month, and I recognized that this man deserved reliable transportation. He recently borrowed a beat-up car from a coworker. So the first thing we did together as a couple in month one was to buy him a truck. I needed Joey prepared to help with the hustle of my busy world with children. He was my lifeline.

"Don't worry, my credit is excellent, and I have car insurance for our new truck."

He moved in that first month, and I graciously helped him grab his limited belongings from his rental. He lived there with a woman that I never saw. So I was a team player when I walked into their main bathroom and started deep cleaning it. Nobody had kept up the bathroom, and I scrubbed away at the mildew of his previous life.

"Erase the old to make room for the shiny new" seemed like a good mantra to repeat while I cleaned.

..

Even as my 40th birthday edged closer on the calendar, I still hadn't been exposed to much death. I had attended a few funerals and was still very uncomfortable with my emotions when I saw the family or listened to the celebration service. The heart-crushing weight I experienced, regardless of my relationship with the deceased, made me feel weak when I looked around the room and found I was more emotional than many people in attendance.

My Aunt Jenny wasn't well. Her life choices weakened and damaged her body beyond repair. She spent her last days in the hospice ward of our local hospital, and I faced my fears of "showing up." I wanted to do more than simply visit on her last days; I needed to be genuinely present. The emotional intensity of hospice was unfamiliar to me as I watched family come and go. I paid close attention to how each managed their flood of feelings. I did not run. I felt it all.

I tackled this emotional mountain head-on and never looked back. I knew showing up for a dying family member was what my parents couldn't do, so I wanted to do it better. Those brave enough to sit in the room had conversations about dying and love and loss, which were beautiful. Then, with my raw emotion fragrant with the smell of death, I walked to her bedside and watched the last of her life unfold before my eyes. It wasn't easy.

For her funeral, I walked in with Joey by my side and felt so much comfort. My parents and I were still uneasy, but we had been trying to work out our differences. With plenty of family members to sit next to, I took the more uncomfortable choice and willingly sat at the table with my parents and sister's family. I made it through that funeral without feeling alienated.

..

A couple of months into our blissful new chapter, I was surprised that this hard-working superhero forgot to pay me the rent for two or three months. The weight of the bills sat heavily on my shoulders, yet I struggled to use my voice and speak up. By the time my anxiety drove the bus, I felt financially overwhelmed and desperate.

"It's been a couple of months, and you haven't given me money for the mortgage."

"Well, you haven't reminded me."

"Didn't it seem obvious that your checkbook held extra money?" said my silent inner voice.

I had taken half a year off from teaching for the birth of Camille. My taxes looked different, with another dependent and half of my regular income. I celebrated that my sacrifice to stay home with her rewarded me with a very healthy tax return. My financial windfall temporarily placed me at ease. This single momma of three daughters drove an hour each way to earn a wage that set me a few hundred dollars above the poverty line. Money mattered in my life, whether I had it or I didn't. A scarcity mindset is what I knew.

I may have had a partner to come home to, but my life didn't always seem more manageable. I brought expectations into our relationship and didn't offer much room for negotiation. My anger flared when Joey was supposed to pick up the big girls after school, but instead, he went out with coworkers to drink.

"How could you let them down? Didn't you feel a sense of responsibility?"

My unhealed narratives around alcohol rushed to the surface; I yelled a lot, and I even shoved him.

My thoughts screamed without following through, "I expect you to be the new father figure in their life. You will NOT choose irresponsibility over them. They already have a real father that let them down."

A red flag waved inside me, but I ignored it.

Life shifted three months later. Joey was living in my little bungalow and driving the truck I had purchased with him. Work required him to travel to the west coast for a week, and I would be back to managing a near-impossible schedule alone. That one week turned into two, which turned into almost three—the responsibilities of a one-year-old and two middle schoolers sunk me. My superman wasn't available to help.

He returned, and I craved reconnection and help. The victim needed her wounds licked. I needed validation that these past three weeks had been difficult and inconvenient for us.

"Share in my misery, please!" I thought.

I needed to say, "I just can't do another unplanned leave of absence from you."

Joey resisted putting much salve on my wounds. However, this trip gave his ego a booster of validation and worth. He felt underrated as an employee, and this trip proved his hard-knock education was enough to earn respect.

The reconnection I craved never occurred. Instead, I felt a noticeable shift in Joey's demeanor as I leaned against the kitchen counter and drew him to me. He was distant and lacked interest in me; he wasn't trying to hide it.

My heart felt bruised as I said, "I am sure you are tired. We can reconnect after you rest up."

Our relationship changed after that three-week trip. I clung tightly so more distance wouldn't form between us. The honeymoon phase ended, and we shifted into "family" mode.

..

My parents celebrated Camille's first birthday with us at my home. We held a quiet, disgruntled acceptance of the status quo of our relationship. Two months later, the pendulum swung swiftly in the opposite direction. The bruised egos and emotions we swept under the rug must have popped out. I never knew what to say or how to act when I was around them. It made me feel strained and exhausted. I was a part of the problem, but I didn't know what role to play to make this relationship easier. On this particular March day, I entered my sister's split-level home with my baby in tow, ready to celebrate my sister's birthday. I climbed the steps into the living room, and tension hit me square in the face.

"Oh, no. It's going to be that sort of day. I wonder what I did," my chest tightened.

I felt like an unwanted guest. My parents and I didn't greet each other that day, and we shared no words during the three-hour gathering. Instead, all parties stood toe to toe and dared the other to break the silence with a pleasantry. Mother's silent treatments were not new to me, and my mind knew how to reach a level of paranoia. The back of my neck felt tight and tingly while pressure built in my chest and throat. My brain's attempt to control the situation went into high gear, and I tried to determine what I had done wrong.

"Should I say something? I just got this larger tattoo - was that throwing them off? Had I missed calling Mother back when I said I would? When was the last time I spoke to her, and how did it end?"

The hours of discomfort ticked by, and we distracted ourselves with the children in the living room. As little Camille crawled on the kitchen floor, Mother stepped around her as she held my baby nephew. This grandma offered no acknowledgment or greeting to her granddaughter; she ignored her.

My heart was screaming, "Who the hell ignores a beautiful baby? I don't care how uncomfortable I make you - she is innocent!"

She received smiles and interactions from my brother-in-law's dad, and I was so thankful for his loving heart. At least she didn't feel completely isolated from love in that house.

..

Joey and I ventured to Vegas right after his return from the West Coast. It was my first trip to Sin City, and I was ready to experience the bling and splash. I was already considering this trip as a chance to reconnect with my Superman. Unfortunately, we had shifted off track, and our energy was stale and strained. Since his return, he hadn't invested effort into helping us feel like a new couple.

"Hey, Heather! Do you see the red flag yet?"

We had a good time, and the bling of the city did not disappoint. Las Vegas felt like an adult Disney World. Oddly, we visited and explored the tourist attractions and didn't gamble a single quarter during our vacation. It was a much-needed time away, but it didn't feel like a new relationship honeymoon. We sat in a bar for five hours and watched the college basketball playoffs. Joey and I discussed the topic of elopement, probably during commercial breaks. I focused on the details I wanted to hear and ignored the rest.

"I would elope with you," echoed and kept pressing Joey to talk more.

If he married me, that would get my life back on track! I would feel stability.

"Should we have Leif fly the girls out here this week and elope now?" I asked.

It was a lot of fluff talk, but it was what I needed to hear. This man mentioned marriage, and I took the bait. Months after this Vegas chatter, nothing had resurfaced about getting married. He settled into my home and life, and Camille grabbed onto him as her father figure.

"What was the holdup?"

As we camped over the Independence holiday that summer, I pressed him about marriage. I started the conversation by speaking plainly; I wanted answers.

"So are we going to get married, or what?" I asked.

"I can see us getting married on New Year's Eve or Day," he offered.

I locked onto this timeframe and thought, "See! He wants you. Your next chapter will have all the features of the past one, only better!"

I was so desperate to get married because I feared Camille's dad returning. When we started dating when Camille was one-year-old, Joey made it clear that he wanted to adopt her. My fear that Wells would stroll back in was unmanageable. Camille had called Joey dad since she could babble anything that sounded like words. Within weeks of meeting her, he bought Nike baby clothes and shoes, and she started to look like she was his. I gave my baby away to this man because of fears about a different man. Joey didn't need to pass a test or prove his integrity; my anxiety and weakness opened that door and let him walk in.

..

After having Camille, the stress of being a single momma, paired with postpartum, had me spiraling. I accepted the six-therapy-session offer from the hospital and had my first worthwhile therapist experience. A warm blanket wrapped over my shoulders as she tried to calm the shivers inside me. I wanted more than those six sessions, but that was the allotment. By this time, I had tried several therapists with similarly flat results. Connecting with Tracey post-delivery was a gift on many levels, as I also had a renewed faith in talk therapy. One year later, I searched for a new therapist since I continued to experience body image anxiety. My body, relationship with food, and lack of self-love created severe instability. I wanted to find a therapist to help improve my self-worth after the devastation of my partner's lack of interest in me. The stars aligned, and another angel stepped into my life that offered what I needed. I entered her office and talked about my relationship with food and my body, but we didn't stick to that surface topic for long. She saw right through the mask I wore. It took little effort from her to release the dam of trauma that had built up for decades.

My new therapist's name was Missy; she was magical inside and out. Her eyes saw me and she was the most present a human had ever been with me. I knew she valued my health and well-being and I offered her my trust. Together we uncovered my festering wounds around my parents and Leif. I wasn't fully aware of how much I carried in my suitcase of avoidance and denial, but we started to dig through the baggage. As a certified EMDR practitioner, she suggested I take a metaphorical step back from some of my trauma. Healing would happen if I could separate those traumatic experiences from the core of who I was.

Eye Movement Desensitization and Reprocessing Therapy (EMDR) is an evidence-based practice used to treat trauma and PTSD. Missy navigated this eye movement process with me only a few times. Still, the long-term impact made a tremendous difference in my ability to release some of my tightly held-traumas. During our sessions, I didn't feel a shift in my perspective as I processed. It wasn't magic hypnosis that worked with the snap of the fingers. Instead, I would wake up the following day and feel like a switch had flipped.

I retaught my brain the messages I desperately needed to believe, "These experiences do not define me. I am allowed to feel the pain. I am worthy of love."

I worked through the mud and muck of my deepest wounds. It was challenging! I left sessions with Missy with a tear-stained face and her directives to "take it easy" the next day or two. My past experiences had a lock-tight hold around my heart, and I needed to keep stepping forward. I kept clinging to the belief that one step forward was better than staying put or stepping backward. I looked at some pretty traumatic memories with more self-love and care. These sessions were just as much about my parents as they were about Leif, which surprised me.

"We accept the love we think we deserve."

Missy helped me recognize the many layers that threatened to suffocate me.

..

My cozy bungalow needed to be bigger for two adults, three kids, and a cat. So one month after Joey moved in, we started to look for a more significant house. My realtor friend, Polly, never voiced any concerns about my house hunting with someone I had just met. She had helped my desperate attempt to purchase my Glenwood home only two years previous. That cute tiny home meant a lot to me but not as much as orchestrating the vision of normalcy and safety I craved.

We found a home thirty minutes closer to my teaching job that fit our needs. Camille was 19 months old; she played in the moving paper and boxes as I gleefully packed for a better chapter. I painted a fresh coat on the Glenwood walls and placed this little sanctuary on the market. It sold quickly with a cash offer. Unfortunately, on moving day, the old wedding dress was forgotten in the garage's rafters and left behind for someone else to discard. As Joey and his son, Thomas, carried my prized kitchen hoosier out to the moving truck, the brittle wood twisted and tumbled. We could not salvage this sentimental piece of furniture. The real pain came when he grabbed the upper portion and tossed it onto the nearby garbage pile. He felt no attachment to it and junked it like rotten fruit on the counter; I cried over the loss.

..

I earned $25,000 to invest into the new home from the sale of my last one. I was solo on the mortgage and title for the new residence, but I needed Joey's financial help to afford the upgrade. I willingly donated all of my profits to update and improve our new dwelling. I invested the Glenwood winnings on shiny, new appliances, Amy Butler wallpaper, and many gallons of paint. We converted the wood fireplace to a gas one and purchased a beautiful farmhouse table and ginormous hutch. Money wasn't a concern, and I bought everything I couldn't afford before Joey. By the end of summer, we invited people over for a tattoo-housewarming party. I welcomed this public display to convince our people (and myself) that my new chapter was right on track.

The party for our friends, coworkers, and close students was a successful event. We had great food, tattoos in the backyard tent, and many laughs. We sat around the fire pit with the tattoo tent still lit and abuzz behind us. As afternoon turned into evening, the adults had consumed enough alcohol to turn the jokes more colorful and tactless. In a matter of minutes, the hauntings of my past appeared in the backyard of my new life. To an audience of friends and students, Joey jokingly told the crowd that he was going to take me upstairs and "fuck my brains out." The humiliation and mortification were all too familiar as I became the subject of this sexually toxic comment. My students witnessed the degradation while I said and did nothing. Voiceless.

..

Joey had been there for Jenny's passing the previous February, so I didn't have to attend her funeral alone. I was thankful for his support. That August, we lost my Grandpa. He spent his last days exactly where he wanted: in the home he built. Grandpa had muscled through cancer and lost his voice box for the last dozen years. His laryngectomy may have compromised his ability to live the life he loved on the water, and he struggled to maintain his gardens, but he still stubbornly lived out his last days on his terms. Grandma held off his celebration of life for two months and honored him at a large family gathering in their backyard. With the leaves in full glory at the end of September, we met to celebrate three lives: grandpa, my grandma's 85th birthday, and the birth of a new great-grandson. It was a true circle of life. We sat in the backyard under a canopy to honor Grandpa. Tears flowed freely when Leila and Rose sang a song, and their youthful voices filled the air. Each grandchild placed a flower in a vase to salute his green thumb. Throughout the afternoon, family and friends shared memories and stories, and we chuckled through the pain.

Joey lent me that supportive arm I needed. One row in front of me sat my dad. He held a white handkerchief to catch the tears falling down his cheeks as he said goodbye to his father. He did not have his partner's support at his ceremony. His wife (Mother) of 40 years chose not to attend because she knew that I would be there; her oldest daughter made her too uncomfortable. She couldn't find enough courage to honor her father-in-law nor support my dad as he said goodbye.

Her absence was evident to everyone. It was anxiety-inducing and painful. The birth of Camille had not been enough to mend the rift with my parents. The death of Grandpa did not help draw us closer. It seemed like our differences were insurmountable. I cried that day for my grandpa and my dad, and the utter sadness I digested knowing my Mother couldn't be in my presence. I felt orphaned; my worth was questionable.

..

The months and years ticked by as Liz (my best friend from my first teaching job) and I embarked on new paths. We no longer possessed the synergy of the foursome we had been for over a decade. She found her footing and came out of her trauma fog; I kept one foot in and one foot out of the shadows of my past. It took her 18 months to drive the two hours to see my new home. With every phone call, she made numerous promises to visit, but her actions didn't bring her closer to me. I slowly started to understand that we were losing our connection. I knew we had both gone through a lot, but I didn't want this friendship to change. I was not ready to give her up; my heart needed her.

..

After a school day in September, I motored over to a local gun club. This Momma headed to the shooting range to watch her eldest daughter shoot trap. Michelle had become a rising star in the trap world, and it was a joy to watch her in action. So many versions of Heather showed up when I drove into that parking lot and saw the circle of humans gathered to support Michelle. The first antagonist was my father, who stood beside my abusive ex-husband. The third member of this group was my current partner, Joey. The three men stood together like they were friends. My self-worth and value felt defined, "Not one of these men is willing to stand separately to support me."

My dad knew how Leif treated me, but that wasn't enough to prevent these bonded outdoorsmen from staying buddies. I wasn't worth protecting or standing up for, and that dagger pierced the deepest parts of my heart. A new nervousness percolated as I watched Joey stand beside the men who had both hurt me so profoundly. Yet, this story felt normal to me, so with the slight slam of the car door, I walked the dirt path toward the men in my life as if it was all acceptable. I took my place in the circle and tried to focus on supporting my daughter, yet inside I was mad at all three of them! I was also furious at myself for being willing to walk up and stand next to these traders.

"We accept the love we think we deserve."
..

Running was no longer my exercise, but I actively tried to control my weight "problem" with vigorous cardio workouts. After a handful of intensive cardio days, my neck started to feel tight and angry. I was no stranger to neck pain, but this felt different. No amount of ibuprofen, massage, or rest helped ease the stabbing pain. I even hung upside down over the edge of the bed to reduce some of the pressure. Finally, I woke up one morning as pain shot down my left arm. I couldn't ignore the issue any longer and went to Urgent Care. As an odd coincidence of timing, a chest spasm happened right when the nurse asked questions of me, and more swift action started. I wheeled into the emergency room to begin a long series of tests. I wasn't having a heart attack but needed an MRI. After five hours in the ER, I learned three things:

I had significant degenerative disc disease and would need to see a neurosurgeon. That information was scary. The neck pain I experienced was the pinched nerves between my deteriorated discs, which was unlikely to improve.

The MRI also revealed I had a previous stroke. They showed me the dead brain matter that looked like a stone wedged in the mushy gushy of the back of my brain. I recalled a scary event I endured after Leila was born that had paralyzed half of my face and throat. Nothing had shown up on the MRI then, and the medical team had concluded I had complex migraines. Nope, it had been a stroke. They assured me that my body had already compensated for the damage at the time of injury and that I would experience no future side effects.

I had sat alone all day in that hospital room, keeping in touch via text with Joey. When they were ready to discharge me, I needed a ride home, but he had driven in the other direction to run basketball practice. Luckily for me, my daughters were worried about me, so Leif brought them to visit. Finally, my ex-husband got me to the pharmacy and home, over 45 minutes from his home. I am thankful that he helped on this day, and it probably helped that I was drug-induced and could accept his offer.

Joey returned from practice late that night, and I was more than ready to talk and receive comfort. We spoke for less than five minutes, exchanging pleasantries and concerns over my medical day. Then, he put his shoes on without sitting next to me in the living room and announced he would work in the garage.

My heart heard, "Heather, what you went through today wasn't all that much. So why did you think you deserved comfort? Chin up, girl!"

I lived in an oxycodone coma for the next month, which wasn't all that bad from what I can remember. The never-ending, aching pain in my neck that traveled down my arm made me depressed, and I struggled to get to work for months. The drugs helped keep my sanity but made my reality a foggy haze. The neurosurgeon said I needed a double neck fusion at C4-C5-C6. There were lifting restrictions after a neck fusion, so Camille was a significant factor in when I could schedule surgery. She would need to be out of her crib and have more independence with her car seat. I needed relief from the pain and a break from the oxy, but meeting Camille's needs was more of a priority.

There was an additional struggle happening off-stage. My fifth year at Floodwood High School had a significant uptick in stress level.

A new principal led our district, and the transition was bumpy. Our union was working full force, and I was a leader on the executive committee with many responsibilities. Stress hit me from all angles: my career, body, and relationship with my partner.

While all those pieces fell apart, I obsessed over marrying this man. I believed if that one union took place, I would be released from my past and secure with my future. We had discussed a New Year wedding, but no proposal came my way.

"How am I supposed to start planning this New Year wedding if you don't freaking propose!"

Fall gave way to snow and busy days filled with drama directing, teacher negotiations, doctoring, and basketball coaching. I accepted that the wedding would not happen on New Year, but I was devastated and borderline paranoid. His excitement about us and this chapter had fizzled as life continued with the day-to-day.

..

Discussion about our union didn't happen, yet the conversation about Camille's adoption did on many occasions. My fear of Wells' return to stake his claim with our daughter (regardless of his being MIA for almost two years) disabled me. This fear haunted me enough to bring up the sensitive topic of getting married, although I was fearful of that conversation too.

"I thought you wanted to get married at the New Year. Why didn't we?" I asked.

Joey said, "You didn't bring it up."

"Isn't it your job to propose?"

Blah, Blah, Blah, Blah excuses. Where he waffled with getting married, he was just as steadfastly persistent on adopting Camille. Why was he eager to adopt her but not marry me?

"You can't have her before me," I said with more neediness than I liked.

Only a few months later, in the early months of 2016, I sat at the familiar mahogany table of my lawyer. This gentle giant remained true to form and sat with his sock-clad feet up on the desk. I guess he didn't like shoes. I hired him to discuss the adoption process to sever Wells and allow Joey to adopt her legally. But unfortunately, the meeting didn't have the conclusion we envisioned.

"A judge isn't going to go for this," said my lawyer. "Why would a 50-year-old man want a baby when he isn't even married to the mom?"

This handsomely paid, shoe-discriminating lawyer refused to move forward with an adoption application. Did I recognize the over-sized, crimson flag waving in front of my face? Nope.

Instead, I thought, "Joey, did you hear that? For our dreams to come true, you need to put a ring on it!"

I figured now he saw the well-lit path. Heather as his wife, would equal marital bliss AND the ability to adopt Camille.

Months went by with no discussion and no wedding proposal. Joey offered no playful hints or twinkling in the eye that he had any intentions of popping the question. My nerves were strung as tight as steel strings. I received no gifts of love on Valentine's Day from the man I was devoted to; he said it was too difficult to buy for me. I could not "hear" the messages he sent me daily.

..

The stress at school was off the charts, and employee morale was in complete discord. I worked with my therapist, Missy, to weather these emotional storms more frequently. At school, I felt tremendous pressure and was targeted by the administration as a union executive. The emotional strain I felt within my home and school walls led to many sleepless nights. Missy offered me the support I needed and a comforting shoulder. She wrote a letter defending my mental health and extreme stress and suggested I stay home for the remaining school year. It simply waited in her folder in case I needed it. I felt like I was at rock bottom, but knowing she wrote that letter and was ready gave me the courage to finish the school year.

I couldn't return to Floodwood the following school year if I valued my sanity, and this decision ripped open a gaping hole in my heart.

These students and this building had been my home stability when most things had crumbled around me. Leaving was devastating, and I grieved deeply. I cried with students every day for the last month as we mourned the upcoming changes. With only a couple of weeks left in the year, my goal became to make it through the Class of 2016's graduation.

..

The end of the school year was days away when Joey and I took a weekend and ferried to Madeline Island. I should've been relaxing as we enjoyed the late spring breeze and a couple of beers from the upper patio. Instead, I was frustrated and edgy. We had been together for over 1.5 years. I owned the vehicles and home we lived in, even though he helped with the payments. Why weren't we getting married? In the end, I forced the issue and conversation.

"Shit or get off the pot, Joey," was the romantic message I delivered that Saturday to my partner.

"So what do you want?" he asked.

"I want to get married. There is no reason not to."

He paused. I don't know what he thought during those moments of silence. Maybe he understood that his comfortable life was on the line. Perhaps he considered what life would look like if he denied me this request. But, on the other hand, he was probably tallying a mental pros and cons list.

"Well, I guess we better get you a hippie ring."

That was his concession. He agreed to marry me, which meant I got what I wanted. No wave of joy or relief surged through my body as I had expected. I knew this was a forced union, not the type of love I deserved. My fear of being alone spoke much louder than my need to feel warm and fuzzy. Part of me believed that being a hopeless romantic was a load of crap. THIS is real life.

We returned home the next day and posed under a tree in our front yard. Our engagement picture and announcement were posted on social media and looked like the blissful celebration I wanted. People congratulated us, I picked out my hippie ring, and wedding plans commenced. I assume the wedding ring went on my credit card.

..

With more job experience, I found a new teaching position for the upcoming school year without a problem. I still felt slighted by what had happened in Floodwood, but my pride drove me to prove I was a good teacher. I took a risk when I accepted a position only a few communities away, but part of me thought there would be enough separation. However, I believed in my ability to teach and connect, so I led with that focus and aimed for a fresh start. My new position was at an alternative school that brought students from multiple surrounding districts. I became the 7-12th grade English teacher for this diverse population.

An alternative learning center is an educational intervention to support at-risk learners. Students that benefit from an alt-ed program have had academic or behavioral difficulties. What I immediately loved about this educational setting was the value placed on the relationships with students. I still taught strong content, but there was an emphasis on supporting students with their challenges. This philosophy resonated with me. I found an educational platform where connecting and guiding superseded test scores.

..

Around the same time I connected with Joey, Liz found a man that seemed a good fit for her future dreams and plans. My heart rejoiced as her social media posts had her smiling again. We were both slated to be married a few months apart in 2016, and we marveled at the similar timelines.

That summer, I took a best friend, Trisha, to Liz's wedding in Southern Minnesota as my plus-one. The grandiose barn spoke of vintage charm with lace and architectural delights. The happy couple took pictures with their new family, and all three children looked like angels. As Trish and I took seats in the upstairs barn, we waited for the ceremony to begin. I recognized and greeted many people that I knew from the past years. As more people streamed into the space, it became apparent this was not a small or intimate event. Liz's past four years had been challenging, and everyone embraced this new chapter for her. The audience's energies bubbled with anticipation as we watched the wedding party begin the procession.

The ceremony began as the bridesmaids walked down the aisle: one, two, three, four, five, six, and seven. Seven bridesmaids announced the bride's entrance. Elizabeth looked beautiful adorning her father's arm as they walked down the aisle. Their ceremonial message braided together love, second chances, and faith. My heart truly rejoiced for my friend.

Another emotion washed over me as I watched Liz's ceremony. Yes, the barn was over 100 degrees this summer day, but something else pressed down on my chest. I felt it but couldn't quite identify the strain. After the ceremony, people mingled, ate, and drank out on the lawn and in the decorated barn basement. Trish and I stood behind the happy couple as we waited in line for dinner. We shared excited congratulations and hugs, and I welcomed this first moment to connect with my best friend.

I thought, "Am I being overly sensitive, or did seeing her not calm this disease I feel?"

The bridal party performed a synchronized dance on the barn floor during the reception. I watched the group of ladies dance and laugh and finally understood the weight I had felt on my chest, "I don't belong." That beautiful bride was once my person, the one I considered a soul sister. But unfortunately, I hadn't received the memo warning me how significantly our relationship would change.

I couldn't dig into those feelings, but that didn't stop the swell of anxiety that rushed in. My stomach dropped, and tears threatened the back of my eyes. Trish and I left without saying goodbye to create our fun night elsewhere. The next day we drove four hours home with the Jeep top down, blaring 80s rock. I played the music loud to drown out the uncomfortable thoughts that wanted their stage within my head. I just couldn't go there yet.

Later, I let those thoughts have a voice, "How did I not make the top seven people in her world to stand up at her wedding?"

The pain festered. I still wasn't ready to change or give up our sisterhood, but something had seriously shifted. Had I been holding on too tightly? My relationship with Liz had never been an issue before, and I grieved the changes. I trusted I could be honest with her, so I sent a message. I prayed she would be willing to receive my message and listen as I shared some intense hurts. I had high hopes we would work through this and find our stability.

"Wasn't my pain and loss done for a lifetime? Hadn't I cried from the actions of others enough? I picked the scabs off my desperately trying-to-heal heart; I wanted to believe I could be worthy of some-one picking me. But, who was interested in choosing me because they couldn't imagine a life without me?" My victim mentality drove the bus into a complete tailspin.

A much quieter voice cleared its throat to speak up, "Isn't it time to consider what you need from the people in your life?"

I couldn't have predicted the outcome as my bleeding heart placed a boundary with another human I loved dearly. I needed to stand up for myself and my heart. I came to the table and vulnerably showed my love and pain, free from bitterness. Her response was also sincere, but she couldn't quite understand the depth of my hurt, and I didn't feel seen. It wasn't enough.

I closed our text and friendship with, "The loss of our friendship is just one more thing those unhealthy boys took from us, and that breaks my heart."

..

Joey and I set the wedding date for five months later, in October. I kept the ceremony and party simple yet meaningful. I could handle most of it independently but required him to do a few things. As the wedding date neared, we needed to be ready to apply for the marriage license. I was dumbfounded as I watched Joey drag his feet on the renewal of his expired driver's license. Applying for our marriage license had a timeline; the longer he dragged his feet, the edgier I got.

"What the fuck? Just do it already!"

I put on my big-girl panties and forced the issue (I was getting good at this). Joey admitted that his driver's license had been revoked before we met. It hadn't expired; he had just never reinstated it. So for over a year and a half, I paid the vehicle insurance for a man with no license. Joey firmly believed the charges were bogus and that the sheriff was an asshole.

"I didn't tell you because I knew you would be upset because of your past with Leif." he deflected.

"I think I deserved to be the judge of that. I paid to insure you."

He continued to divert his responses back to the weak and damaged Heather, that never would have understood. The more frustrated I got, the more he felt my irritation proved his point. Ultimately, he had to renew his driver's license to apply for our marriage license. The fines got paid, his license was reinstated, and our auto insurance policy delivered a hefty increase.

I had regular conversations with myself as I tried to sort the baggage, "Was this a part of getting my life back on track? Does this feel good?"

One week before the wedding, we arrived at the courthouse to officially declare our intent to marry. We stood behind the solid oak counter and completed our written request. The nondescript woman behind the bar looked over the completed application and took her notes.

"Is this the 2nd marriage for both of you?"

"Yes," I said.

"No," Joey said.

Time paused as the air rushed out of my lungs. I couldn't breathe. I turned my head to look at him as he answered, "It's my third."

I was going to be his third wife. Am I not his second? Who else was there? What was even happening? These thoughts loudly rallied around in my head, and I couldn't make sense of them. Now the spotlight shifted to me. The government worker took in my body language as I slowly placed distance between myself and my fiance. I inched down the solid countertop as I digested the news. I had many questions but wallowed in the awkward silence and said nothing. She took this as her cue to move forward with the application.

"Please raise your right hand...."

She continued to read, "Do you solemnly swear that the above information is true, according to your best knowledge, that you are single and unmarried and may lawfully contract and be joined in marriage."

My voice was a mere whisper as I answered, "Yes." His oath was the same.

My legs walked me to our Jeep, but I was on autopilot. Tears started falling down my cheeks before I fastened my seat belt.

"Who else were you married to? Why didn't I know about her?" I asked.

He met my emotional distress with his frustration and anger.

"I didn't need to tell you because it didn't matter," he said.

I argued otherwise, "It does too matter! You misled me into believing Haley was your only other wife! I don't like being blindsided by this!"

The conversation ended there because neither of us had anything more to say. I did not receive an apology, but I also didn't push the pause button to learn more details. Instead, we drove home and fell back into the momentum, launching us toward the wedding only one week away. A new mantra repeated in my head, "One week. One week. One week. She calls him daddy. One week."

..

This 2nd wedding was the one that I thought was the "real" one. My first marriage had ended so brutally my romantic heart believed it must have been a test run for something even better. However, with all the family drama over the past few years, I found it uncomfortable to plan the guest list. Family squabbles suspended so many of us in limbo, and I wasn't confident about who to invite and who to pass over.

My therapist, Missy, asked me two questions about those people: "Are they in your life now? Do you see them in your future?"

These questions cut through my emotions, and I could think objectively. Joey and I created the guest list and left off the people that I couldn't answer yes to. My parents did not make the cut and wouldn't be included in my wedding celebration. The venue was a coffee shop in an ornate historical building that had been a city jail. It was a romantic, non-traditional venue decorated with bohemian mismatched trinkets and books.

I couldn't contain my nerves on the drive to the ceremony to wed my partner. My anxiety had been through the roof all day (which surprised me), and I listened to SNL Presidential debate clips of Trump and Clinton for distraction. Finally, I impulsively put on the brakes and made my cousin-chauffeur stop at a bar moments before walking down the aisle. I hoped one or two shots of tequila would steady my tremors.

Our closest friends and family stood up next to us. Little Camille, looking like a princess in her floofy dress and floral crown, held our hands as a cousin officiated the wedding. I read my carefully written vows and reflected on our journey to find each other. I vowed to share the very best pieces of myself with him without hesitation. Then it was Joey's turn to share his vows with me. The words he spoke caught me off guard. He talked about how people mentioned having hope and wishes and how he was different.

"I don't have hope."

The negative vibe made me squirm, and I felt embarrassed as we stood with an audience.

It was uncomfortable until he switched gears and said, "I don't have hope because I KNOW."

He said this forcefully, and I saw our officiant grin and exhale. I hadn't exhaled, yet she pronounced us husband and wife; he dipped me backward and sealed it with a kiss. So we were officially Mr. and Mrs. Lange.

The rest of the evening was a small-scale celebration with family, friends, and students. A food truck parked outside offered "His & Hers" meal options. We served homemade wine with labels that proudly displayed our two Jeeps. My dress was gray, flowy, and unique. My friends had decorated the venue with books, hippie bohemian fun, and coffee shop ornamentation; it screamed the eclectic designs of Heather. These details came together to create a festive, flavorful event worthy of a wedding reception.

As my tired and blissful body started climbing into our bed that night, I discovered the cat had peed on my side. A karmic message, for sure. The marital bliss expectations fell short when my new husband didn't feel the need to make love - or any form of intimacy - on our wedding night. We didn't make love for a couple of days. Intimacy had resorted to begging on my part, and I didn't want to be whiny the first week of our marriage. I had what I wanted, right?!

One month later, I succumbed to a knife to my throat. The time was right for my long-awaited neck fusion. Camille was almost three years old and more independent; the time had arrived for much-needed relief from my chronic pain. My neurosurgeon cut the smallest incisions on my throat to access the C4-C5-C6 region behind my windpipe. I woke up with a drainage tube out of my neck and a fancy three-month accessory (neck brace). Being a little eccentric, I decorated the hard-shell neck brace and the softer brace with pretty scarves to disguise their obviousness. True to prediction, this fusion did the following:

It immediately relieved my arm pain.

The fusion limited my ability to tilt my neck forward and backward by 20%.

It failed miserably to diffuse the neck discomfort.

It wasn't until a year later that I purchased an inversion table. This flat tipping board locked you in at the ankles, so that you could invert and hang upside down. As my body was suspended upside down, I could feel my spine lengthening in the opposite direction, releasing compression. This beautiful beast helped me relax my spine and ease the tension in my neck. That table is truly orgasmic and has given me more sighs of pleasure than any man.

..

After marrying Joey, Camille's adoption was full steam ahead. Wells waited until the eleventh hour before agreeing to sign over his legal rights to her, but in the end, he did. On February 21, 2016, Camille became Joey's legal daughter and earned her new name: Camille Lange. I felt tremendous relief that the monster I believed to be breathing down my neck had signed off, and I could release that fear forever. I could never have fathomed that I had traded one monster for another.

I settled into my cookie-cutter, double-income household with a partridge in a shallow-rooted pear tree. We carried on in the usual way. I finished my Master's degree in Education focusing on Character Education and was proud of the accomplishment and pay raise. With the extra funds that came in, we celebrated with more travel time. Joey and I went to the Big Apple and Broadway, which was a dream of mine. New York is rich in history, culture, and art and did not disappoint. We also brought the three girls on an RV road trip across the country to Niagara Falls. We looked like a scene from National Lampoon's Family Vacation as we drove across the countryside and the kids rolled around on the back bed. We dipped our fingers and toes into the Great Lakes and landed on the Canadian side of the falls. It was a great vacation, but I could not deny my unhappiness.

..

I used to count the days that lacked an intimate connection between us. Weeks would go by with little to no interaction.

"Why isn't he interested in me?" haunted my thoughts.

I was neurotic and wanted our intimacy and connectedness to improve. At this point, any intimacy shared was pity sex. Joey blamed it on age and diminished sex drive, and I asked him to go to the doctor.

Unfortunately, he wasn't too concerned about getting help in this area. I begged to be touched for over a year when being intimate didn't appeal to him. Never once did he give me what I requested. My feminine identity was shaky after my marriage to Leif, and Joey's tight control over my sexuality crumbled any remaining foundation.

..

Peculiar dreams haunted me at night during this chapter of my life. As with most of my dream patterns, I always disappoint someone with missteps or failures. This narrative circled in my sleep for over two decades without lessening. The dreams I recycled during my relationship with Joey were particularly terrifying. I dreamt of forgetting to care for a baby or a pet at my home. My body filled with dread as the severity of the consequences became apparent, even in my dream state. A mass would form in my throat, and I would taste bile as I realized I'd find them dead in the walls or a dark closet. The waves of horror suffocated me as I continued the scene and told the parents that their child or pet was dead due to my carelessness. I would never be able to remove myself from this shame and guilt.

I asked, "What kind of person forgets or abandons an innocent baby?"

The only answer that came back was, "Me."

..

I witnessed new levels of student trauma during the year I taught at the ALC. Their experiences revolve around addictions, violence, homelessness, and extreme behavioral outbursts. Most days carried an undercurrent of tension felt by everyone. Yet, there was also a vital joy factor when walls came down, and a smile emerged. These students' life experiences could bring full-grown adults to their knees, but they still showed up.

My angel friends heard about the high need and often donated money and food for these students. During Valentine's season, we purchased new socks, wrapped each with a pretty ribbon, and passed them out to the students. More than one student immediately removed the current pair and threw it in the garbage. Students beamed about fresh socks; it doesn't take thousands of dollars to make someone's day.

"There are no lions in this place" was my classroom motto.

Whatever chased them outside would not be allowed in our room. That classroom was designed to make students feel safe and supported; it is where I encouraged growth, healing, and learning. Once I established trust, I knew we could start focusing on education.

One upperclassman said he had never read an entire book. I challenged the 11th and 12th grade English class to read *The Kite Runner* by Khaled Hosseini. This complex text was a stretch for many students as they read about a foreign culture with a new vocabulary bank. TT was challenged with instability and homelessness and brought those experiences into the classroom every time he made it to school. Still, he stayed committed to reading that book. Sometimes he read the paper copy, and other times he listened to the Audible app. He finished half of the book at the end of the unit, so I tested him only on that half. I gave him the same high-level assessment as the other students, earning him a solid B. Success. In traditional classrooms, this is a failure. I refused to look through that lens. TT did what he could with what he had. He read a complex text, and he was able to demonstrate what he had learned. Life isn't white picket fences for everyone, so why do we give assessments like it is?

I created a last-hour-of-the-day art therapy class. Students were exposed to various creative outlets: painting, nail art, cross stitching, bullet journaling, slime making, and painting by number. I joined them in several activities and felt myself unwinding at the end of the school day. Students learned that creativity could be an outlet for processing big emotions, thoughts, and energy. There was a lot of pride in that classroom with their creations.

My emotional scars from the last district faded, and a new type of joy emerged from being a part of this school. I took a step back and saw that I needed this new educational scene to better myself. I had not planned to leave Floodwood, yet now I felt like I was even closer to my calling. I was still edgy and anxious around power struggles, toxicity, and injustices and tried to walk and talk a quieter path. I assumed that would be enough to keep me under the radar and out of trouble.

I was so thankful to be away from last year's toxicity that I turned a blind eye to what was happening at this new school. Instead, I grappled to understand the crass attitude of my new principal, who also happened to be a woman. Our team would meet with students and parents for an intake process before admittance to our program. Part of our leader's sales pitch boasted that this school was here for students who needed a space to feel comfortable.

She always added, "Our teachers are the same. They didn't belong anywhere either."

After I had heard this commercial a few dozen times, it rubbed me wrong. She downgraded and labeled us misfit teachers. It was hard to hold my head high at those moments.

During our regular team meetings, her vulgar sense of humor ran unchecked. "Fucking bitches," is how she referred to us in those meetings as she pretended to be the voice of a student. Our team was called "cunt" twice and told to put on our big girl panties and fix our team differences. Once, she even called my classroom phone heavy-breathing like a stalker. But, for the record, not one student ever called me a fucking bitch or a cunt.

I tried to block out the noise and drama from our school leader; I was committed to my job and students. With only two weeks remaining in the school year, teachers and students scrambled to tie loose ends. Our teaching team experienced some discord that affected students, and since our principal had told us to deal with drama on our own, I sent an email to a teammate to find a resolution. I know how to use precise language and be professional without being offensive. I asked for clarity in this email and suggested we hold a team meeting. I kept it factual and positive. That email backfired and lit a ginormous dumpster fire I could never have predicted. My coworker took that email to our principal and formally complained. Our leader called me into her office the following day before school.

My principal said, "Who do you think you are for sending that email? You are the most toxic person in this building, and I don't know if I will hire you back next year."

She said she would consider my future employment over the last two weeks of the school year. So, with that kick in the ass, I started my teaching day.

I met with the Superintendent and a union representative (even though I didn't have union rights during my probationary year). I laid it all out. I shared a handful of details from the year.

"As a professional woman and educator, I don't appreciate being called a "cunt" or a "fucking bitch," no matter what the context is," I said with as much inner strength as I could muster.

I told this high-level administrator I loved my job and the students but wouldn't return next school year.

"I quit."

As I exited her office with some dignity, I said, "I plan to have a conversation with our student population. I need them to know that I am not abandoning them because of anything they did."

I shook her hand, and I walked out.

I told the students I was leaving. I cried. I discussed the importance of staying healthy and happy and spoke about self-worth. They understood that my departure had nothing to do with them and that I could not work for someone that saw me as the most toxic teacher in the building.

In hindsight, I probably shouldn't have been so transparent. These kiddos were full of energy, passion, scars, and pain. I should've been able to predict an unpleasant outcome, but my anguish clouded my judgment.

The students revolted. A bunch of girls went to find the principal to "talk." One boy got in his car and drove laps around the block, pointing his middle finger out the window at the school. The situation imploded, and I knew it couldn't get any worse.

The teaching team gathered the students and talked everyone through the challenging thoughts and feelings. Finally, students returned to a better level of calm, but climate change came too late. My principal saw red, and there would be blood paid. Within the hour, the principal and superintendent entered my class and escorted me out of the building.

"Give us your laptop and keys. You won't be returning for the rest of the school year. You will collect your items after the school year is over."

I exited the building and walked the streets of town, completely bewildered. I was broken, confused, embarrassed, and shamed. I sat at a local coffee shop on their front porch and waited an hour for my husband to come to pick me up.

"Was I even a good teacher? Was I toxic? Was I damaging to students? How had my intentions gotten so misconstrued?"

The main question I wanted to answer was whether or not I was meant to be a teacher. I honestly wanted to run into the wilderness to lose myself, bury my shame, and hide from the finger-pointing.

..

Michelle and Leila had experienced a lot of inconsistency and trauma in their early stages of life. I carried a lot of guilt for my part, wishing I could have shielded them from the pain. I craved writing new, happier stories with the two of them. We weren't covering up the past; it was about the importance of showing up today and finding joy despite the history. For each girl's Sweet 16 birthday, I took them on a Momma-Daughter long weekend trip in an attempt to manifest positive intentions.

Michelle and I went to Chicago in August for a sunny, memorable retreat. We flew. We toured. We Ubered. The Windy City shared its Chicago dogs with us, and we experienced the Shedd Aquarium, Field Museum, Willis Tower, and the Broadway performance of Hamilton. The weekend boasted our independence, where the ghosts of our pasts were not invited.

A year and a half later, I flew to the West Coast with Leila to experience Seattle, Washington. We shopped at the Fish Market, visited
the original Starbucks, luxuriated in a spa day, and snowshoed Mount
Rainier. We walked downtown Seattle searching for the iconic Grey's
Anatomy hospital, circling and retracing our steps. The locals must
have shared many laughs as they watched the dopey tourists searching
for a fictitious hospital - I'm sure we weren't the first. We made special
memories and experienced the freedom that travels offer.

"Yes, Girls, you are strong enough and smart enough to travel,"
Momma said.

..

With my revised resume, I initiated another search for a district
to employ me. I had left two schools under stressful circumstances the
past two years and felt defeated. Was I even worthy of teaching anymore? The stars aligned, and soon after walking out of Virginia, I was
lucky enough to find another teaching job in a district closer to home.
At the interview, I learned the job would not be content specific (such as
teaching English). Instead, this program offered one last opportunity to
seniors that didn't have enough credits for traditional graduation. My
new position would focus on reading, writing, and math skill building,
financial literacy, career and college exploration, and social-emotional
support. The program was specific to Wisconsin, but I understood this
population of students well and was confident I had found a good-fit
position. I felt like an at-risk human myself.

Superior High School was my first large-district employer. Fear
of larger-than-life expectations had prevented me from applying seriously to these larger school districts. However, immediate advantages
became evident with more support systems and improved structures.
There wasn't pressure to take on year-round extracurriculars or to
chaperone every event. My new district empowered each professional
to find balance. What a land of beauty! My previous notions about a
large school district had been entirely off base. I might have liked being
a large fish in a small pond at the other schools, but that hadn't served

me well. As the new school year and position unfolded, I learned my program was an island within the vast waters of the high school. Most staff members did not know the specifics of this program, so I received limited outside influence. Anonymity was mine! I had space to teach, heal, and thoroughly learn the program's specifications. I became a small fish in a big pond, and I loved it.

The seniors that entered the classroom were similar to my previous ALC students. I understood this population. I had a toolbox already set up to guide them to the coveted diploma, and a lot of it focused on developing relationships and trust. It took the first year to understand this state program's nuts and bolts, and I am thankful for the great mentor and vice principal who was my resource. His patient guidance allowed me to fall into this role while considering adding and strengthening the offerings. Two Iron Range school doors might have slammed shut in my face, but the Universe opened a better one for me in Superior, WI.

In seven short years, I had been in three different schools with three different positions and followed six lead principals. Yet, the root of each was similar: my job was to guide, teach, and mentor young adults as they decided to enter the young adult world beyond high school. I helped them, yet I am forever grateful for how much they healed me.

..

The end of 2017 was another dumpster fire of upsetting and unfortunate events within our household. As my marriage deteriorated, I could not handle the reality of another unhealthy marriage. I had regular appointments with my therapist, Missy, since I was a born-again believer that capable professionals did exist. She heard my frequent marital concerns and recommended we see a top-rated sex therapy couple to work on our intimacy disconnection. I thought that was the root of our unharmonious marriage. Joey surprised me and agreed to attend marriage counseling, so I took that as a win moving us in the right direction. His other option was to listen to this unhappy, unhealthy, sexually deprived wife. This highly qualified, married, interracial couple met with us three times.

I wish I remembered the specific details of the first two meetings. The male therapist immediately developed a man-crush on Joey and took over my nickname for him, Superman. This professional team looked at our issues differently than I expected. Joey's surface-level answers appeased them, yet the therapists weren't taking my concerns seriously. Over and over, my objections and defenses were deflected or dismissed.

By the third session, I understood that I had lost. As someone that asks for clarity, I looked at both therapists and said, "What I hear you saying is that I expect too much from Joey. I need to lower my expectations for our marriage?"

I asked this calmly and without bias. The wife looked at me, nodded her head, and verified I had heard correctly. They both believed the expectations I placed set him up for failure.

Her husband saw his opportunity, "You are the one closed off to him. Look at you on the other side of the couch with your arms crossed across your chest. You are sending such a message."

His description was accurate. I was closed. I wanted to crawl into a corner away from Joey, and I didn't feel any differently about this therapist. My skin felt like it crawled. Therapy had been my idea to get our marriage back on track, not to damage my self-worth further.

He continued, "I am more worried about your mental health. You have cried this entire session. Are you on any medication? If so (not pausing for my answer), it might be the wrong dosage."

His eyes roved past me to Superman, "Joey, we cannot change someone's reality. So if Heather comes to the dinner table thinking she is Santa Claus, we just accept that as her perception."

No noise escaped my throat as the tears continued down my face. I had just wanted to try to mend our broken intimacy. Instead, I felt so alone and defeated.

"We accept the love we think we deserve."

"We accept the love we think we deserve."

"We accept the love we think we deserve."

I walked outside the business building that brisk December night and uttered, "We are never going back there."

Joey just looked at me before we parted ways to our separate vehicles. I started the engine and allowed it to warm as my fingers dialed the number of the person I needed. Missy answered my call, validated my pain, and scheduled an appointment to see me the next day. Unfortunately, those credited marriage therapists significantly damaged my already bruised soul. Even the best-trained people fall prey to a well-versed con artist.

..

One week after that final therapy session debacle, Michelle received a threat from another girl from her high school.

A freshman texted my sophomore daughter and told her, "The next time I see you, I'm going to kick your ass."

We met with school officials to review what happened until the text and how to proceed. Michelle admitted her fears to the Dean of Students and the Liaison Officer. This threat fell into a gray area since the text was sent off the school campus, paired with the inability to confiscate the student's phone. The school's administration didn't take the situation very seriously, and we left the building to wait for an update on the actions taken. I took Michelle home with me for a much-deserved personal day. The follow-ups from the school were meager, and nobody initiated a plan to get Michelle back into the classroom.

"Aren't they going to do anything, Momma?" asked my sixteen-year-old.

I felt as flabbergasted as her, along with some momma-bear offensiveness. I reached out to other professionals within the school system and advocated for my daughter, who still sat at home self-learning—days ticked off. New information came to light that the bully had bragged she had unknowingly cut Michelle's hair in the hallway. My blood pressure ticked up in elevation, and I climbed the educational food chain for answers. My calls made it to the school district's Assistant Superintendent before someone promised action.

The bully stopped texting her (she had a conversation with the administration), but because of the district's limited action and support, Michelle wasn't willing to return to that school. Her one mental health day turned into six weeks of at-home learning before educators and students began to use technology effectively. She spent her days at my high school, in my classroom, and brought her assigned work. The semester came to an end, and Michelle somehow maintained her A-average. However, the school lost her trust, and she chose to transfer to a different high school midway through her sophomore year. Life isn't always white picket fences, even for sixteen-year-olds.

..

A family crisis deployed the last bomb of 2017, one week after Michelle's text threat in the middle of December. I was invited to a close family member's for a visit before the holiday with the understanding she had information to share. The reasoning was vague, and my mind searched to fill in the blanks. I sat on her hardwood floor with a fire in the stove to my back and waited for her to share whatever news she had. My eyes met hers.

"Heather, your life will never be the same after you hear this."

She spoke concisely, and it only made me more nervous. The only logical topic I could muster was a divorce between her and her husband. It was much worse.

"Child molestation has happened within our family," she said.

I didn't understand. My cousin told me the rest of the details, and my body went numb. All I could do was lay back on that wood floor for support. Specific stories hold such horror that the body has a plentitude of physical reactions from the tale. These aren't stories we want anyone we love to tell. To add another layer of bewilderment, my own Camille was close enough to the perpetrator that there were questions to be answered on our end. Still overwhelmed with emotion, I drove to Joey's work to tell him of the charges. His fatherly instincts immediately kicked into high gear; where I felt sad, he felt anger.

A realization formulated in my heart, "Our family will never be the same again."

Our extended family had their way of dealing with the information, as denials and alliances formed. As the fissure widened, members of the family jumped for positioning. My mind reeled as aunts, uncles, cousins, and even Grandma picked their side. Unfortunately, something that seemed black and white didn't draw predictable results. Most family members were content to hang in the messy middle and "not believe" that the perpetrator could have done something so horrible.

"Oh…there is no way that Stanley did that," Grandma said on our one phone call after the news came out. "Maybe it did happen to [the child], but I know Stanley didn't do it."

"Grandma, why hasn't anyone reached out to support the family if you believe it might have happened?" I cried out.

I needed her to see where our family was failing. But unfortunately, she didn't have an answer to my question but tried to hand the phone over to one of my aunts.

"No! I don't need to talk to her! Grandma, what if this happened to Camille? This is the type of support we should expect?" I pleaded, hoping for a different outcome to the conversation with my matriarch.

First Witness, a child advocacy center, advised us how best we could support Camille "in the event" she had been a victim. It is safe to say that she was not, as no red flags arose to suggest otherwise. However, I still couldn't remain indifferent and needed to cut cords with any family member who did not support the victimized child. The state stood by the child. I stood by the child and their family. This trauma demanded I sever people I desperately loved from my life (and my daughters'), but I didn't see another option. Sometimes a situation has a right and a wrong, and people have to pick a side.

Before 2020

"Fear, uncertainty & discomfort are your compasses
toward growth. We must let go of the life we had planned,
so as to accept the life that is waiting for us."

– Joseph Campbell

..

One other Lange man impacted my life; Joey's young adult son, Thomas, lived with us part of the time we were married. This young man had gentle, playful eyes and a soft heart. He had a snarky wit, and we bantered well. He lived with us for a time and helped drive the big girls to school. I thought of Thomas when I planned a menu or stopped at Sam's Club. This tech-geek foodie became an adhesive in my marriage to his father. For months, Thomas and I joined forces publicly and privately to poke fun at the fearless Lange leader. It empowered both of us as we were stronger together than alone when we dealt with Joey.

Despite the closeness I felt toward Thomas, it was challenging to have another adult in the household while we experienced severe marital tension. I felt embarrassed. This union was relatively new, and it was already on the rocks. I didn't hide my unhappiness well, and it came out freely in my joking with Thomas. Joking could sometimes mask turmoil.

One evening after I drank alone, he came home from a night out. We were both buzzed and loose-lipped.

"Things are not going well with your dad. I just wanted you to know that we probably aren't making it. I will wait until the big girls are done with high school in a couple of years to do anything about it," I shared.

"Why wait? Leave now. He won't change."

Thomas's blunt response caught me off guard. We weren't joking anymore. I defended the situation and argued the big girls deserved stability, but my answers fell short with dull sadness.

He continued, "What do you expect when you are wife number four."

I simply stared at him. My mind replayed and caught up with what he had just said.

"Heather, it's time to find your voice. Speak," my mind screamed.

"What do you mean... the fourth wife?" I stammered.

My stepson seemed oblivious to my confusion, "Well, I have stood up for him at three weddings."

We needed to be on the same page. Yes, his dad lied to me until the week before our wedding. The memory of learning I was wife number three was still reasonably fresh. My brain ticked off some quick mental math.

Thomas's face displayed disbelief and understanding as he watched me, registering his statements. The mood of the evening drastically changed within minutes. We cried. We hugged. We took a subtle step back, and both acknowledged the unspoken truth of imminent change on the horizon.

After that, there was no going back. Thomas' admission removed my veil of naivety, and the red flags I had seen the past three years formed one large, red blanket of truth. The old familiar shame and fear rose up and nearly suffocated me. I was back in another deep, dark hole in a world that I had created. I just hoped I was strong enough to find a way to climb out.

I found the three previous wives from an easy court record search. I printed off the proof and waited in our living room for Joey to arrive home from work. I bubbled with an emotion-laced cocktail of anger, disappointment, shame, rage, and sadness. I handed him the printout with various marriage dates and wives. I watched and waited as he read its contents. We stood at a crossroads and would not be traveling together moving forward. I had accepted so many inconsistencies in exchange for security. Joey folded the paper in half and handed it back to me.

"So what," is all he said.

I returned the gaze and enunciated each word, "We. Are. Done."
..

Joey seemed relaxed as we completed the state's do-it-yourself divorce paperwork. His peaceful acceptance of our failed marriage was uncanny, like a business deal that didn't come to fruition.

"She takes this. He will take that. Check this box. Sign here," the documents urged without emotion.

Our divorce was scheduled for the end of May, only a few months away. I felt so blindsided by the truth that I obsessed over the possibility of more unknowns lurking in Joey's closet. How had I not known? I became my private investigator and contacted the other women who came before me. Connecting with them offered some soothing comfort just knowing I wasn't alone; they all had ridiculous stories and experiences with Joey. While I spoke to wife number three, she unearthed another new morsel of truth. Joey had a son over in Sweden (can you hear the screeching tires as my brain slammed on the brakes?), and she thought the boy's mom was named Andrea. This information would seem preposterous under different circumstances, but I figured anything could be possible. Local public records were easy to uncover, but I had no idea how to investigate this new international suspicion.

The gears in my head started to shift and grind, "Grab it, Heather! Grab it!"

When Joey and I moved to our new Pike Lake home, I had designed his & hers stencils of the cities we had resided. I had intentions to paint the signs for our covered porch. Joey had included the town in Sweden where he lived while he served in the military. I had ordered that stencil over two years ago but found it tucked away in my craft files. Land sakes, how lucky!

There on the stencil was the name of a city in Sweden. I knew it was a long shot to sleuth out a woman and young man across the world. So I did the one thing I knew worked to connect people, and I logged into Facebook. I searched for Andrea Lange's on Facebook in that Swedish town listed on Joey's stencil. I found three women matching that name in that town.

I wrote the same introduction to these faceless women overseas, "Hi! I am trying to find an Andrea Lange who was married to Joey Lange."

Three hours later, as I sat in the dining area of a Perkins restaurant, I received a reply from one of my inquiries. SHE had responded.

With the answer to a random Facebook message, I became wife number five. I wasn't wife two or three, as believed in 2016. I wasn't number four either, with the information Thomas had provided only weeks prior. I was wife number five. I had stopped feeling unique to Joey long ago, but these secret wives felt like an extra kick in the teeth.

Andrea shared her tale of emotional struggle with her son's father. Not only had Joey abandoned this baby when he was a year old, but he had also not granted her a divorce for eight years. Ultimately, her country gave her separation from him and dissolved the marriage so she could move on. Joey had not waited to unite with wife number two, but that is a story for a different wife and chapter.

The layers started to fall off my tattered soul, revealing a new truth: "This 'man' had adopted my daughter!"

I needed to stand sovereign and muster every ounce of my courage. So, with shaking fingers, I made two phone calls: the first was to the courthouse to cancel the upcoming divorce, and the second was to a legal office to hire a lawyer.

..

Names hold meaning. Often our name is a big part of our identity. One of my favorite authors, Diane Chamberlain, wrote posts using nicknames she assigned to her husband and children. I thought it was so personal how she showed each of them, "I see you!" The creative in me followed her lead and coined names for my three daughters: Independent Warrior Daughter, Musical Passion Spark, and Fierce Little Angel. I used them playfully like a secret code, "Your momma sees and loves you!"

My girls remained solid in their nicknames and birth names, while mine changed with the tides. My vision as a younger girl was to keep my last name until my prince charming arrived and offered me his. We would live in marital bliss behind that white picket fence. Unfortunately, the search for myself through the years had come with more name changes than I was comfortable with.

I had never liked my maiden name simply because people couldn't pronounce it. When it was called out by a teacher or a doctor's office incorrectly, I was the one that felt second-hand embarrassment when I had to correct them. I was more than happy to offer it up when I married Leif. When we divorced 13 years later, the girls were still young enough that I wanted to keep the family name the same between us. Over a year later, when I got pregnant, the value behind my surname was placed under a spotlight. The baby's father had his surname, but I wasn't sure he would stick around. After much contemplation, I returned to my maiden name to share with the upcoming baby. I have to admit, I asked Leif if I could give the new baby the Stevens surname so that all three girls could connect by name, and he offered me a resounding, "Fuck, no!" I had to ask, right?

I tried to overlook that my surname connected me back to my parents, if only by six letters. I received so much love from my grandparents and my aunt, who had the same surname, so I leaned into those feelings to feel like I belonged with that family. A man with the last name Lange hoodwinked his way into my life and married me, so I took his name. After we married and he adopted Camille, she took his last name. I learned about many women with the Lange name from his past, and I couldn't remain in those statistics. I wouldn't go back to my toxic surname, either.

My identity crisis began, "Who the hell was I?"

My feet rested at Cyndee's crackling fireplace as I lamented my situation.

She looked at me and said, "So, make up your name. Who are you?"

Cyndee challenged me to think outside the box yet made it sound as easy as announcing my favorite flavor of ice cream.

"I don't know who I am! I don't know where I belong," my heart cried.

I didn't see this as a solution right away, but she pointed to a worthy option to consider.

"Invent yourself, Heather. Don't worry about belonging to any tribe but your own," she ended our conversation.

My love for naming things, from children to cars to sewing machines and bikes, guided my way, and I set out to discover my own identity and who I was. I also needed to figure out who I wanted to be.

I made lists of names for a couple of months. I researched the word origination, along with my intuitive rumination. Post-It Notes littered my spaces with different versions of my potential name. I clung to this quest as if a treasure would be waiting at the end of the rainbow once I made my final selection. I needed a name that defined my past, present, and future to come. Then, when it came to me, I did not doubt that I had "found myself."

Here is my surname manifesto:

Wilde

Wilde, Wilder (def): Germanic Origin. to lose one's way, untamed, indicative of strong passion, desire, or emotion, deviating from the intended or expected course

Laura Ingalls Wilder - the beloved books & Tv Show

Oscar Wilde - "Be yourself; everyone else is already taken."

Gene Wilder - Willy Wonka and the Chocolate factory. Floodwood. Kiddos that changed my path forever.

Wild: from lost to found on the pacific coast by Cheryl strayed - she had a symbolic name change and published a gritty, powerful memoir

Into the Wild, The Wild Truth: Chris and Carine McCandless' quest for self and truth

Heather Wilde - online search. She is called the "unicorn whisperer." That is good enough for me.

The mirror reflects my image - the face I have recognized as my own for 43 years. Life has offered more creases, grays, and insight. My eyes are wide open, but I still feel something is missing. Don't most people find comfort and safety in their name? I can't be the current Heather Lange - that name doesn't hold truth, even if it belongs to my little one. My surname is tied to generations of psychological wounds that included some that have left permanent scars on my heart. There is still a 3rd last name in my past that belongs to another story and my two eldest daughters. These names do not identify the woman staring back in the mirror.

My new name is like a gift, a rebirth. It magnifies my inner strength and independence. My hero's journey has developed me. With this identity, I am committed to the search for inner peace and joy, to stand proud in my skin, and to share my compassion with all. I offer a new path for each of my daughters that demonstrates the need to always be true to yourself. I own my past. I appreciate each tear I have shed and each decision I have made. I am passionate. I am free from constraints. I am Heather Nicole Wilde.

"Loving ourselves through the process of owning our story is the bravest thing we'll ever do." Brené Brown

I stared out over the cliff's edge and felt Joey's betrayal in my bones. The truth had swiftly removed so many layers, and I was off balance and paranoid. I agonized over possible unknown details. I was confused about how to proceed with a custody agreement. I embod-ied tremendous mom guilt for the interrupted life my older daughters faced again. My heart shattered on a perpetual basis as I considered what this meant for Camille and the man she knew as Daddy. Those emotions smothered me daily, and I felt frozen in the circumstances of my life.

As the hurt subsided, I felt resentment boil up inside of me. Don't misunderstand; I still felt like a victim. The anger became stronger than hurt feelings, and I firmly believed it was all his fault.

"Why was I the one relocating? Hasn't enough trauma happened already in our lives? Who the hell was this man?" all ran around in my mind.

As the former wives and children came out of the woodwork, even former girlfriends reached out to connect with me. I was dumbfound-ed. How could Joey have walked over and through all of these people? When he omitted this information from his story, he stripped me of the right to decide if I wanted him in my life.

One thing was clear, "If I had known any of this, Joey would NEVER have been allowed in my life - not on a date, not in my home, and not in the lives of my three daughters."

..

Fear couldn't silence my voice, and I called out quite literally. I called our city police, the county sheriff, and a probation officer friend, and they all answered me with similar reactions: disbelief and fascination. None had advice for me.

"Wow! I have never heard a story like that," they said, "It sure sounds wrong, but I am not sure if Joey broke any laws."

"Thank you. I am aware I belong on Dateline."

Another phone call invested without justice, but I didn't give up. I just changed the scope of my search. My quest took me across the bridge to the neighboring state and county, where we married. Again, I spoke to multiple people, shared my suffering, and hoped someone would do more than sympathize. I am an educated, well-spoken, and persistent person who needed great feats of tenacity to keep pushing forward. I needed someone to look deeper into my story and validate me. I called over half a dozen people until I found one person willing to chat a little longer and offer me hope. I received a return call from the county investigator, and a smile formed as tears of gratitude fell. The evidence was pretty simple: Joey lied under oath at the courthouse the day we applied for our marriage license. That, my friends, is a felony.

..

A part of me wanted to fight tooth and nail to take back Joey's rights to my youngest daughter. Yet, the only time his eyes welled with emotion was when we spoke about the custody of Camille.

"Don't take her from me," he said.

This rare show of emotions didn't pull on my heartstrings too much. I had shed enough tears, and his red eyes meant very little to me. My investigative work continued as I researched how to rescind an adoption. I spent my free time searching for justice. Finally, I found an adoption attorney for the price of 35-50k who would dig into Joey's original adoption application process to see if any of it had been falsified. She spoke honestly and said the chance of success would still be slight. I didn't have the money or the drive left in me for these types of odds. The only facet of this custody I could fight was the time he was allowed with her. Camille was four years old and loved her daddy very much. I didn't see a gray area within the scenario: I needed to allow the space for a healthy relationship to be fostered, or I needed to fight to keep him out. I swallowed the most significant lump while handing control to the universe. I couldn't fight this scenario any further and refused to use Camille as a pawn. I would agree to his having equal custody without argument. Deep inside, I had to trust that a much bigger power would hold her up and protect the journey with her dad.

..

I was open to any activity, practice, or friend group that led me in the opposite direction of most of my previous life choices. An opportunity arose to participate with a group of spiritual women holding a Cacao, Despacho, and Qoya dance ceremony. I knew some ladies in the room or had heard of a few others. Each component throughout the evening nourished my soul with healing waves, starting with selecting an Oracle card calling us from the floor. As I explained to the group why "Queen of Self Discovery" was an appropriate card, the tears started to fall unchecked. I was certainly in a phase of self-discovery. A Shaman opened the ceremony with Cacao and explained the drink's intentions to help us become self-aware, allowing our wishes, hopes, and dreams for a better future to bubble up. She spoke soothing balm for my soul, and I accepted the invitation.

The Despacho ceremony is a South American tradition of offering gratitude and positive intentions back to Mother Earth. We created a prayer bundle with elements from the Earth that were individually selected and blessed before being added to the center offers. It felt much like we were creating a natural mandala. As I took my turn in the center, I emotionally made my selections and added them.

"I offer seeds as I set my intentions to plant anew, bearing a new kind of fruit. I am choosing coffee beans in gratitude for my energy. Lastly, I offer grains of rice, representing my daughters. Please hold them closely and support their every need."

I bowed and wiped my eyes and nose before returning to my space in the circle. Later, the bundle was gathered and tied up to be planted into the soil of the Shaman's land. I wholeheartedly believe Mother Earth heard and received our gratitude and requests.

The last part of our ceremonial night was the Qoya dance. After feeling wrung out, dancing and physical expression seemed overwhelming until I learned Qoya was the simplicity of free movement. That room held each of us as we enjoyed sensual motion and recognized the physical sensation of truth and bliss in our bodies. That's when "she" showed up. I smile now as I remember my inner child taking physical form next to me, wanting to join the playful dance. I had never seen her before; tears rolled down my face as I held her hand and twirled her around. Her long straight hair flew out as she smiled and giggled during the dance, simultaneously reminding me of her meaningful existence. She wanted a place in my life, and I wanted nothing more than to allow her that.

..

I needed a vacation, mostly from my life, but the state would be a good start. The past few years had taken their toll, and my inner wanderer needed to leave the area. Part of me wanted to outrun my pain but already knew that wasn't a possibility; no matter how far we drove, the dark pieces inside us came along for the ride. Seclusion for a week sounded divine, a location where nobody knew my name or my life story.

"Fuck you, Joey. I am going on a vacation alone, and I will enjoy my own company better than I ever did yours," I thought as if he cared.

I called a travel agent and shared my cravings. I handed over the planning reins and gave her full authority within my budget. With the divorce in negotiations, I had Camille stay with her dad and the big girls stay with Leif so I could take this trip alone. My agent sent me to a bougie spa resort in Paradise Valley, Arizona, at the beginning of July. The sweltering heat didn't matter as much when the fragrant pink flowers tickled my nose as I walked the resort. I had never been to Arizona, and the view of Camelback Mountain took my breath away. I settled in for seven nights, eight days of rest and rehabilitation, and strong intentions to find myself.

During the first 24 hours at the resort, I grieved. I sat by the pool and let my Minnesota body acclimate to the desert heat. I drank cucumber jalapeno margaritas and ate nachos and wings. At one point, I moved to a bar stool next to a tattoo artist and booked an appointment for some impulsive trauma therapy at the end of the week. As the sun faded behind the mountains, I cried in the pool. A towel at the pool's edge soaked up my tears and muffled my sobs. I didn't hold back. I allowed the overpowering shame and sadness to come out, and I wailed.

The following day I felt cleansed from the previous night's release. A patio breakfast inspired my soul with black coffee, an inspirational chakra book, and free-flying little birds. I dove into that chakra resource and searched for answers to my chaotic life. There were answers in that book. I felt like a sponge, desperate to soak up any wisdom or knowledge that might get me on a better path. The root chakra resonated the most with its common feelings of unworthiness, insecurity, and fear.

The questions poked at my wounds, "Did I truly love myself and believe I belonged here? Did I feel worthy of others' love and joy?"

I devoured that book like a born-again Christian reading the Bible. As I continued reading, my eyes opened to the many spiritual parts I had been ignoring and needed healing.

My vacation formed a pattern of healing, reading by the pool, visiting the spa, and pretending hard that I didn't mind being there alone. I only ventured out of the luxurious resort for a one-day tour of Sedona. As I rode in a small tour bus with other tourists, I felt increased anxiety and worry. I had left the safety of the resort and sat amongst people who all "had someone." I felt more alone and small than I had since arriving in Arizona. There was no running back to the resort to hide, so I put that mask more firmly in place.

"I feel totally at peace and content being on this bus tour alone," I tried.

Sedona was one of the most spiritual locations in the United States, nestled in the majestic Red Rocks. I shopped, took a canyon jeep tour, and had my previous wedding ring cleansed by a Spiritual at a crystal shop. That ring had stood for so much. Tears slid down my cheeks as they performed a ritual to cleanse the ring. They gently returned my item and suggested I wash in the waters of nearby Oak Creek if I had time in town.

The last event of Sedona day was a tour around the town. Our guide drove us past homes of the rich and famous, the Chapel of the Holy Cross, and an outdoor amphitheater. We were allowed an extended stop at one of the vista vortices, where I sunbathed in a tranquil rock garden built by past visitors. I cried out to the Spirit Guides of the Sedona Vortex for answers and knew my Spirit Guides had heard me. Even though it was over 100 degrees outside, I got shivers as I sat in that space and faced my shadows within.

I asked with outstretched hands, "Why me? What do I need to do to escape this toxic repetitive cycle?"

During the 2.5-hour van tour, we drove along the river the Spiritual had suggested I cleanse in. That Oak Creek called out and teased me. I craved getting my feet in its waters to receive a spiritual bath. I couldn't derail the tour, but I wanted in that river. I found my voice and braved mentioning this to the tour guide. As we dropped off the last couple at their resort, the guide turned and told me we had 30 minutes before he had to get me to my return bus. Angels sang, and I smiled.

"Can we go to Oak Creek, please?"

He dropped me off at an access point and encouraged me to take my time. The cement parking lot turned into a grass recreation area, thick with overhanging trees. The Oak Creek ran through the back, and I walked toward it. The sun glistened off the wet rocks and moving water and shined its light on me. I removed my sandals and inched my way into the sacred waters, ready to be cleaned. My ceremony was for one, but I felt my guides and ancestors watch my purification. In the water, I dangled my hands into the current, washed away the old, and accepted all the crap. I acknowledged my role and pledged to search for truth and awareness. While this river wash lacked pomp and circumstance, it was sacred in my heart, and I felt divine calm and connection.

I returned to the tour van, caught the larger bus, and traveled the two hours home to the resort. This day of care was much more than a Minnesota girl who played tourist. I had prepared myself for the Priestess Warrior tattoo I would have inked in 48 hours. Art of that magnitude belonged on the body of a conscious woman.

..

I didn't set out for a new tattoo on my Arizona venture. The decision to boldly ink my shoulder was impulsive with the assistance of some liquid courage. In my inebriated state, I chose the image of a goddess to ink on my body. She was strong, like a warrior with a natural leader aura. I wanted her on my side, literally and metaphorically. I had never studied gods and goddesses and hadn't aligned myself with any deity to guide my way. Somehow one ended up on my body anyway. The artist needled his craft onto my left shoulder for almost six hours on a scorching Arizona day. I watched him become inspired by his work; he transformed with each layer of the tattoo's progress. My warrior tattoo didn't mean this afternoon to be a journey just for me; it was for both of us.

Back home, I told people, "She is the Priestess Goddess, protector of women and children. She protects me, and she is me."

I didn't realize the universe and my Guides listened and delighted in my word choices.

..

I came back from that Arizona adventure refreshed but still vulnerable. That trip wasn't a magic wand that erased years of tragedy. I still WANTED to be numb and distracted. Feelings of unworthiness and victimhood were oddly comfortable for me - I knew how to play this game. I signed up for cable TV for the first time in my life to get lost in the noise of the airwaves. There was an uptick in my substance usage for the first time in my life. When the girls were with their father, I drank 1-2 bottles of wine a night and experimented with CBD and THC; I wanted to feel joyfully numb. I slipped from the empowered place I had found in Arizona back into a more miserable existence. Within that fog, I happened upon the book, *The Miracle Morning* by Hal Elrod. The author had suffered a significant accident and used the book's concept to find purpose and balance while battling depression. I craved predictability and control over something, so a highly structured morning sounded like something I could handle. After reading the book, I selected practices that would honor different parts of my soul every morning.

Following Elrod's plan to begin my day, I brewed my coffee and cleaned my kitchen right up until the pot chimed its completion. I accomplished this simple household chore with habitual movement and without thought. The shortened time limit lifted the heavy resistance I usually felt about tasks because I knew my time would only last until the beep of the coffee pot. I took my steaming mug to my balcony and plant sanctuary to begin the rest of my new practice. I followed a guided meditation for ten minutes and let my brain calm and focus. Now I needed to inspire my heart with words affirming how I wanted to feel, pulling myself out of the mud and muck. My miracle morning ended with journaling on my phone. I often purged dark emotions and toxicity that needed an exit. When I couldn't conjure full thoughts, I simply wrote a list. The magic of wordsmithing became apparent as I watched the pent-up messages pour out.

I learned to embrace the quiet of the morning. The few times I didn't start my day with this practice, I was more anxious and spastic, and my emotions got away from me. There is no better window of time to set the tone for the day. Month by month, this practice became my routine, and I wasn't willing to sacrifice it for an extra hour of sleep. The opposite happened as my alarm clock got set earlier and earlier to allow me even more time to ground myself for the day.

..

My self-awareness deepened as I healed and honestly felt better, but I still lived in an uncomfortable juxtaposition. I had found a big part of myself with newfound independence and strength. Yet, that other side of me still felt alone, abandoned, and craved connection.

I felt enormous pressure when I thought about dating. Deep within me, I felt shame and guilt. I had messed up twice already, and I didn't see how I deserved to continue searching for love. My relational messes were never self-contained and always spilled out onto the lives of the people I loved the most. Due to my dating choices, I had brought pain into my daughters' lives. I intuitively sensed some of my friends' discomfort while others just spoke their thoughts.

"You don't need no man to be happy, Heather."

I just felt so damn lonely. A random guy from across the state reached out on a dating site to chat about my Jeep. My Jeep Wrangler was a man magnet. I answered him with little interest. I admitted to him that I had a fair amount of shit to work through in my life, and he offered to listen out of kindness. I rarely hesitated to share the details of my unjust life, still a well-versed victim. He was calm and grounded, and I liked how he made me safe while we chatted. Even though we connected well, we agreed we weren't interested in dating (more like he told me he wasn't interested). He had three issues: the distance, my young child, and I don't remember the third. We talked for hours and ended it with….nothing. We made no promises to meet or talk again.

The next day we exchanged a simple greeting, "Good Morning," along with the usual pleasantries. He suggested I drive to his hometown later that day, and I was caught off guard. Sure, we had casually flirted, but we had set clear boundaries. All my girls were gone for the weekend, and I accepted without much forethought. I loved a good road trip and wanted to meet the man behind the soothing voice and wise demeanor.

I packed my bags, jumped into the Jeep, and headed southwest.

We met with easy smiles and a casual hug. Brett offered to take me on a boat ride on the lake at his home. The wind blew through my hair as we glided across the water. I felt free. He took me out for a delightful dinner, and we enjoyed each other's company. He saw me... the real me. His passion and bedroom skills caught me off guard. I had never been with a partner who paid that kind of attention to me. There wasn't room to be self-conscious, and I relished the intimacy. The lightning flashed outside, and our energy sizzled.

"I couldn't run to you fast enough," he admitted as he looked into my eyes.

We started an epic summer romance full of playfulness and passion. Together we were comfortable, supportive, and relaxed. I spent all my spare moments at his lake home that we labeled "Camp Brett." I received many gifts from that man as he taught me acceptance of my body and the pure pleasure of being on the lake. Both were life-changing for me. I was finally comfortable in my swimsuit and my body. When he was at work, I was the lake girl with his dog, Buddy. I floated with a book as the summer lake breezes healed me in a way Duluth could not.

Our dating pattern worked that way for over two months. His work schedule made it difficult for him to visit me in Duluth, especially with his dog. That summer, I didn't care if I drove to him every time. When I was at Camp Brett, no responsibilities hitchhiked with me. Summer's end loomed ahead, and I really thought I wanted this to continue. I danced around the topic of getting him to Duluth regularly, but the discussion got uncomfortable, and I would drop it.

As summer drew to a close, my anxiety appeared more pronounced. I needed to know what came next for us - my need for control. The school year would start soon, and my schedule would lose its flexibility. That's when I met the cow. This cow stood in the pasture and chewed with leisure. It saw no reason to budge. Our conversations intensified with emotion. I was blamed for expecting too much or not understanding how difficult it was with a dog. He suggested I was over-thinking, and I argued I wanted a plan.

"You're not Buddha! Quit using 'being in the flow' as an excuse not to make a plan for next month!" I argued.

I also wanted validation that the miles I had invested could be reciprocated when my schedule had to adjust. Just like that, the summer romance ended.

We never said, "I love you." Sometimes I pondered if I felt love or not. We seemed compatible. We shared the most organic intimacy I had ever experienced. Doesn't that equate to love? Unfortunately, those things didn't add up to a worthwhile relationship, and I learned never to underestimate the stubbornness of a cow.

A handful of months later, we reconnected. We flirted. Brett offered to come to see my new home. A few days later, after elevated flirting, He suggested a meet-up. That darn cow appeared, and we fell right back into the same old script.

He lured, "Are you able to drive out to visit me this weekend?"

I came to my senses and realized that great sex might be worth the drive on some occasions, but I had driven those miles many times and was ready for reciprocation. So I passed on the orgasm and decided men could also put in some effort.

..

A wonder powder called Chaga started getting mentioned in my world. It started with two different students swearing at its healing powers. They claimed this natural substance had anti-inflammatory properties and would detoxify my system. There was a lot of noise in the holistic world about Chaga, but I didn't bite right away, especially since the advice was coming from students. Another young adult came across my path and recommended this natural supplement and even offered me some for my coffee. He mentioned its super cleansing powers for my system and spiritual realm. Even my students saw I needed detoxifying, I guess. I didn't believe the trend but caved to peer pressure. With minimal research, I trusted their reviews and added this ground root to my coffee.

I didn't notice any miraculous changes to my body from drinking Chaga. No miracle wave of detoxification or clarity was evident. I added it randomly when I remembered and carried on with my type of trauma-cleansing practices. After a couple of weeks of intermittent use, as I drove my Jeep up Mesabi Avenue in Duluth, I realized I had to go to the bathroom. Having to poop is an everyday life occurrence 99% of the time. My need felt different - there was no significant gut cramping; I just had to GO! As I waited at a red light and planned my fastest route home, without warning, I shit myself. Do not pass go; do not collect $200.

My body decided right then and there that it needed to expel some shit. In my Jeep. Thank all guardians and guides that I was alone in my vehicle. As I parked next to my apartment entrance, I became that waddling toddler with a diaper load as I scampered in. I felt fine afterward and chalked it up to one helluva lousy memory.

I re-engaged in life only to have the same experience repeat a week later. "Ok, Heather, this is not normal."

I went to the local urgent care and signed in, "Yes, my body released my bowels with no warning. I guess you could say I am having problems shitting myself."

A Grey's Anatomy episode unfolded as Doctor McSteamy walked into my hospital room. He laughed with me (or maybe at me). After giving the humiliating details of my shitty experiences, I added that years ago, during exploratory surgery, the surgeon had found an undiagnosed mass between my rectum and uterus. He ordered a CT scan, and the results were clean and contained no red flags. The even better news was there was no evidence of a mass anymore! I celebrated with McSteamy while he signed my discharge papers.

I had left the hospital without a medically sound explanation for my bowel issue. On a spiritual level, I pointed my finger at that Chaga. So much toxicity had built up inside me; I think that wonder powder worked to help detoxify my system. I had much I needed to release, making me shat out the mass. Thank you, Chaga, but I don't think you and I will meet again anytime soon.

..

A 1980s apartment became home after I left Joey. It adequately met our needs, but I drifted and felt aimless. My inner child needed to feel safe and call a place "home." The temporary feel of an apartment couldn't offer me that. We unpacked and repacked from that space in only five months, as I found us a new home across the bridge in Superior. I found the biggest, most astounding 1892 home in Superior. This magnificent corner residence boasted three floors and oodles of character.

"This place must have some serious roots built over 100 years ago!"

As a bonus, if we relocated across the state line, Michelle could attend my high school for her last two years, and Camille would be in my school district. So we hopped the bridge, planted another set of roots, and hoped they would bury deeply and offer security.

..

More women came out of the woodwork and shared their stories of Joey's mistreatment with me. They were a trail of breadcrumbs he left behind in his messy wake. They viewed me as a validation of our shared experience, the same way I looked at them. Ex-wives, girlfriends, and children all had a piece of themselves used or abandoned by this man, and many wanted to speak out. Part of me needed to feel united with a bigger group of believers, and another part felt overwhelmed as I processed my trauma.

I believed in the power of vulnerability and support as we heal, so I formed a "Wive's Club" on Facebook, where each woman had already paid membership dues if this man had negatively impacted her life. We shared and vented our stories, bruises, and scars that spanned over 25 years within the group. We were not alone. An odd kinship formed with these group members, and in that safe space, healing happened.

..

Ironically, I sat before a judge on 9/11 to have the marriage to Joey terminated. My lawyer sat by my side, and two friends sat behind me in support. He sat alone on the other side of the court, without a lawyer or friends. The heavily wooded room fit the mood of the meeting. I felt broken, victimized, and cheated out of justice. Weeks earlier, the judge had requested Joey provide documented data about his former marriages and divorces. Instead, out of defiance or lack of concern, he left areas blank or inaccurate.

"You are Heather's lawyer. You fill it out," was his answer to my lawyer.

I hadn't grown up in a world where people refused requests from lawyers and judges. So I was more astounded when the judge didn't insist he completed the paperwork with integrity. Joey's mishandling of this vital information was THE WHOLE PROBLEM! The mandatory co-parenting class that our state requires for divorces with minors was also not enforced for Joey. He just didn't do it. Instead, he cut corners without consequence, leaving me victimized by our courts.

My lawyer walked through every single detail of our divorce decree. My job was to answer "Yes," for each line. If I chose to disagree, the divorce wouldn't finalize.

My lawyer, "Heather, do you agree that this divorce decree is fair and equitable?"

"Yes."

"Do you agree to have this divorce decree entered as a final solution for resolving your marriage to Joey Lange?"

"Yes."

"Are you changing your name to Heather N Wilde to avoid a felony charge or hide from the law?"

I audibly choked. My face oozed snot and tears without grace.

"No."

"Do you believe the custody agreement to be fair and equitable?" was her dagger to my heart.

I snarled, "Yes."

The court recorder watched and documented my answers, and I read a lot on her face. She knew. This resolution was far from fair and ethical.

..

The dust in my life should have settled by now, but that wasn't the case. Joey and I texted the week before Camille's holiday program, only three months after our divorce. He asked if he could bring a new woman to Camille's program. It wasn't my place to refuse, but I asked for direct answers about their relationship. His tone changed. Joey got defensive and talked in circles about it being none of my business. Two seconds later, he contradicted his litany and told me just to ask if I wanted to know anything. "She" had moved in two months prior (three weeks post-divorce), but he had insisted she was only a friend he was helping out. Her name was Jodelle.

I saw her at Camille's program. We stood within a couple of feet of each other, but I refused to make eye contact. Just days after that holiday program, rumors surged again, and I heard Jodelle might have a ring. I confronted Joey with blunt outrage and argued that I needed to know these types of details to better support our daughter.

He answered, "No, Jodelle doesn't have a ring, and we aren't planning on getting married now." But then, his tone changed to its usual defensiveness, "It's none of your business anyway."

It sounded like living together had upgraded their relationship out of the friendship zone. Unfortunately, direct answers were not a part of Joey's vernacular. I don't think the truth was either.

For Christmas, the custody agreement stated I had Camille Christmas Eve, and Joey had her Christmas day. Since the big girls weren't going to be at my house for Christmas morning, I asked Joey if he wanted Camille later on Christmas Eve so she could wake up for Santa. I would prefer to have all three girls together Christmas morning whenever I could. Unfortunately, our texting fell off, and we didn't establish a time for Camille to be picked up on Christmas Eve, but I figured we could discuss it when the day got closer. Joey didn't answer my text the weekend before the holiday, but I gave it no thought. Camille had excitedly mentioned they were going to a waterpark over the weekend, so I figured they were busy.

On Christmas Eve morning, I texted Joey around 8 am to find out my pick-up time for the day and didn't receive a response. At 10 am, I got the same result. My mind started racing uncomfortably, and pressure started building in my chest. After the third attempt, I understood why I couldn't locate my daughter.

My intuition started to scream, "They aren't even home!"

I called again as bile rose in my throat. This time Joey answered. The noise in the background confirmed he was at a public location, probably not in Duluth, MN.

I barely remained calm as I spoke, "Where are you? I have been trying to reach you for hours to pick up Camille."

"What are you talking about?" Joey argued. "We are at a waterpark 4.5 hours away. She is having a fun time."

Predictably, he became pissed off at me for the miscommunication.

"We aren't coming home until Christmas night. I thought you didn't want her until the 26th," he told me.

Paranoia laced with rage entered my voice, "I never said I didn't want my daughter over the holiday! I sent you a text days ago that you didn't answer."

I cried uncontrollably. I wanted my baby girl delivered to me NOW! He tried a new tactic to guilt me and reminded me that Camille was happily playing at her favorite place on Earth, a waterpark. I was the evil mom who wanted to wreck their holiday. Joey offered no apology or suggestion on how to fix the "miscommunication," so we ended the call. Within minutes I gathered some sense and texted him that I wanted her by noon the next day.

That Christmas Eve was dark as I lay on the living room floor in a fetal tuck. I felt powerless and broken. Michelle and Leila had gatherings they could attend with their dad's family, so I told them to go.

Unfortunately, I wasn't able to fake holiday cheer or entertain them.

That Christmas Eve night, I sent Jodelle a Facebook message, "I would NEVER have agreed to give up Camille over the holiday. Convenient miscommunication. You are a fool for believing his string of lies and considering being wife #6. The truth will prevail. Enjoy your time with my daughter, knowing her mother is sitting home brokenhearted." What a fool I was; she already was wife #6.

The following day I drove two hours away to collect my daughter. Joey dared to suggest he would pick her up later that day as they headed home from the waterpark.

"We are going to pick Camille up when we drive by your home later tonight," he said.

"Like hell, you will. I am keeping her all day today until tomorrow," I snarled.

He tried one more argument, "We haven't even celebrated Christmas yet."

"That doesn't seem to be my problem," I said as I walked away and started the 2-hour drive back home to salvage as much of the holiday as possible.

..

After multiple delays, Joey's case concluded 13 months after the truth had come out. My public defender prepared me for the final session, and I brought a whole section of supporters (including Wife #4). Joey sat alone with his lawyer, without Wife #6 sitting by his side. I was able to read a Victim Impact Statement before his sentencing. As I walked up to the center table with the many-paged speech, my hands and voice shook.

I cleared my throat and addressed the Judge, "I have had many months to consider what I wanted to say for my Victim Impact Statement. In the end, I realize that Joey will only understand from his level of perception. Therefore, I speak these words today for the people in and out of this courtroom, for myself, and closure."

I honored the wives and children that came before me. I told stories to celebrate their journey that had been similar to mine with him. I cried the hardest as I tried to read the paragraph about Wife #4, knowing she sat behind me. Before I could share the second half of my statement, the judge interrupted my speech.

"I don't understand the relevance of this speech," the judge stated.

"Victim Impact Statements can look different ways, Your Honor," the public defender suggested.

"We are not here to go over past scenarios for the Defendant. Please carry on."

The statement I had worked so diligently on wasn't what the Judge wanted, but how was I supposed to know? I stumbled and faltered and said a few remaining words in closing. As I walked back to my supporters, I pasted a smile on my face as if it had gone as planned. I offered validation for the others but spoke no words about my truth. The unsaid lines jumped around in my head and confused me:

I learned so much about self-love after being with you. I am proud of who I became after the shit show you brought into my life. It was all lies – a scam. For the record, I never would have dated you. I would never have purchased vehicles and a home to share with you. I sure wouldn't have let you adopt my daughter or meet my other two daughters. Do you remember Michelle and Leila - the girls who needed a father figure you helped raise for over three years? You lied and abandoned them, just like the other children in your past. You are a poor excuse for a man and father.

Justice served Joey 17 days in jail and a $1000 court fine. The Judge reduced his felony charge to a misdemeanor since he had no prior incidents. Rather than spend those nights in jail, Joey paid an additional fine to wear an ankle bracelet and continue going to work. A year of waiting concluded without much inconvenience for that man, nothing like the disruption I experienced.

..

For the next six months, I lived a reckless life infused with many dates and late nights. Part of me felt empowered to live any old way I wanted. Another aspect of me cringed at my untamed behavior, and self-loathing thoughts would start circling. My worrisome do-gooder would argue with this new "Wilde" child.

"You can't date multiple guys!"

"I can, too, and I will!"

"You seem desperate."

"Who am I even answering to? You? Quit judging me!"

My life didn't have a lot of balance, but I tried to fake it. Even as I bounced from one dating site to another, I knew I wanted a real partner. Almost one year after my separation from Joey, I found myself on a coffee shop date with a different type of man. He was educated and street-smart, financially healthy, and enjoyed the arts. His single pair of chucks and older vehicle suggested minimalism, yet he was economically stable and held a respectable career. I liked the depth of our conversations, and it was a good start. I immediately felt like this one might have some potential.

After our coffee date, we sat on my couch, and he told part of the tale of his past. Pat had an ex-wife and three school-aged children.

"There is some stuff online that you might see, but I wanted to be upfront and explain," he said.

He spun a tale of her craziness and manipulation to explain why she had a restraining order against him. I saw the pain in his eyes. This man wanted to come clean right away, and that impressed me. I believed every single word Pat told me and ignored the obvious red flags he waved.

..

It won't surprise anybody to hear I had serious body image issues for most of my life. Not only had I compromised and defined myself in the name of love, I had also soothed the numerous bruises and burns with the consolation of sweet treats and pizza. My weight and overall shape went up and down just like the roller coaster of my life.

My therapist, Missy, gave me the consistent message, "Your body is simply a vehicle to use. It doesn't define you."

My obsessive body image looping wasn't penetrated by her simple words of wisdom, even though it made sense. During one session, we talked about my cravings for homemade cookies and bars, like I used to have back home as a child.

"My dad had such a sweet tooth!" I said.

Tears started streaming down my face as I made the connection of my intense craving for sweets as a direct link to my dad. Now, as an adult without my dad in my life, baking and eating our favorite recipes helped me feel connected to the relationship we used to have. This was the purest definition for emotional eating, if I had ever heard it.

My chapter with Joey was still unraveling and my pallor, body and mental health all matched in a dingy shade of gray. Two years previous, I had visited a Nutritionist to discuss the possibility of weight reduction surgery. I was tired of trying diets, eating plans, and exercise programs without finding much success. At that appointment, I was advised to gain an additional 20 pounds to be considered. I had felt enough humiliation walking into that office and stepping on their scale; the thought of gaining more weight just didn't make sense.

Last time I had been overwhelmed by emotions I had trained for a marathon. After my neck fusion, I couldn't do that. I desperately needed something to hold onto, mostly to offer me focus and hope. I happened upon just the right human to send me the much-needed inspiration. J and I met through a mutual friend, and we connected right away. They had been on a weight loss journey for around a year, losing 100 pounds. I saw their energy for life with their "before and after" pictures, and I wanted a piece of whatever magic they were casting. J was participating in a structured weight loss program with significant caloric reduction - and it had worked. My eyes grew wide when I learned the monthly cost for packaged meals and coaching, but my desire was so strong. I needed to feel better in the skin I was in.

I started this weight loss journey February of 2019. The first week was pure hell, trying to drink more water than I had before while significantly cutting my calories. My anxiety skyrocketed, I was emotional, and I even came down with a fever (not scientifically linked). As my body adjusted the side effects lessened. By the end of the first month, I was 19 pounds lighter! I was elated at my success and this control calmed my mind as I tried to regain balance in my life.

I stuck to the plan with 80-90% accuracy for almost nine months and lost just over 60 pounds. I didn't look or feel like the same human. I gained physical confidence, found energy, and purchased a new wardrobe. I still had a lot of inner child and self love wounds, but I was hopeful that most of that was behind me. The real questions would be whether or not I could maintain my new lifestyle and size without paying hundreds of dollars per month.

..

Over the past few years, my emotions tended to amp up on Mother's Day as I grappled with the ambiguous loss I felt. As the calendar turned to April and my birthday, I wasn't prepared for those same emotions to gobsmack me on my 44th birthday. It had always been about Her and the abandonment I felt. After a morning round of birthday coffee with friends, a dark cloud descended over me, and I felt my body grow restless. I wanted to leave, yet I had no clue why! No sooner had I started my car when the first tears began to fall. Feelings of bleak sadness and loss followed me for the day.

All I could think was, "I am not worthy of being in my parent's life."

What significance could I possibly have as a woman and daughter, unable to reach that bar; isn't it usually set low? Yet, here I was, on my 44th birthday, questioning my value and ignoring all the beneficial changes I had made to get my life back on track. The force of the emotions was brutal, but it also opened my eyes to the remaining wound that needed more healing.

Around the same time I met Pat, I was actively digging out of the muck and getting refocused on my life goals. I felt even more badass than I had in previous years and felt compelled to explore more spiritual practices. I already had the Priestess Warrior tattoo, understood my chakras, and meditated daily; those things worked out! I purchased a tarot deck from the local mall without considering it. I had never had a tarot reading done for me, nor had I watched one done on YouTube. No tea leaves, palm reads, or spiritual mumbo jumbo had graced this Baptist child's bubble. Now I owned my first tarot deck.

What did I expect would happen with those tarot cards? I laid them on the table, and they told me absolutely nothing. I didn't feel any connection or messages and was ultimately out of my league. I purchased the Wildwood Tarot Deck, which used different wording and imagery than the traditional Rider-Waite deck. How would I know that? I found online tools and classes that helped me some, but I still felt too overwhelmed. I wanted to interpret Tarot like a formula with no room for error - give me some control! So I blocked out any potential intuition and sat there stuck. I am sure my Guides slapped their foreheads and rolled their eyes a few times.

While attending a small spiritual convention with a girlfriend, a vendor presented us with an oracle deck. I hadn't known that oracle cards existed!

"I can feel your strong energy! These oracle cards are an easier place for you to start. Don't give up," the vendor said.

I still didn't understand the concept of intuitive reading. I don't think I even understood the concept of intuition in general. I was most comfortable when I tried to find the "right" answer that matched what I read in the guidebook. I started pulling one card from this new deck, and then I would read the information. I didn't even try to figure out what it might be telling me. The more cards I pulled, the more weirded out I got. How could these messages resonate so much? Their precise meanings left me awe-struck and intimidated. I couldn't explain this mind-reading power and wasn't ready for it. Both my tarot and oracle deck sat untouched on my dresser for over a year.

..

I was satisfied with life. My relationship with Pat had produced something comfortable. We maintained a long-distance relationship (under three hours apart) with balanced visits to our cities. We indulged in the culture of his big city and visited indie bookstores, science museums, and supper clubs. On other weekends we relaxed in the calm of my north woods and walked the beaches of Lake Superior or hiked the many trails. The only wrinkle in our relationship was his ongoing drama with his ex-wife and children. He lamented and commiserated, yet it didn't seem on a trajectory to change. He kept one foot in my world and dragged one foot behind through the sludge of his other world.

The roots I planted at our 1892 mansion proved hardier. Our family was back on a busy rhythm as we kept up with Michelle and Leila's high school events. Volleyball games, band concerts, formal dances, and trap shooting season kept me as a permanent chauffeur carting them around. I spent weekends with Pat. My parents were still not a part of my life, and I had found peace. Even though we overlooked the white elephant in the room (my parents), I had a functioning relationship with my sister's family. My life seemed to have more order than it had in years.

Before 2021

"I knew that if I allowed fear to overtake me, my journey
was doomed. Fear, to a great extent, is born of a story we
tell ourselves, and so I chose to tell myself a different story
from the one women are told. I decided I was safe. I was
strong. I was brave. Nothing could vanquish me."

– Cheryl Strayed, *Wild: From Lost to Found on the Pacific Crest Trail*

Like most of the world, 2020 was a pivot point in my life. Covid was born and reared its ugly head onto US soil. Fear and panic sat heavy in the air as humanity held its breath and drew the curtains. Pat and I had planned a spring break trip with Michelle and Leila to Arizona months before H1N1 was even a thing. As more information about the pandemic became available and our departure date neared, we contemplated if we should go.

News reports with Covid numbers were our drug as if knowledge would offer a straightforward answer about our vacation. Our family sat on the fence, divided on whether or not we should go or forfeit. Minnesota and Wisconsin schools announced their closure on the way to the airport, and our nerves intensified. On that early March morning, we boarded a plane to Arizona and threw caution to the wind. Basking in the desert heat sounded more appealing than returning home to fret. While vacationing, we toured Sedona, Flagstaff, and the Grand Canyon and experienced much of the state's beauty.

I posted on Facebook, "There is no COVID in this place," in the sacred hills of Sedona.

Did I poke the beast? Starting the next day, COVID followed on our heels for the rest of the vacation. Restaurants closed behind us, Antelope Canyon tours were canceled before we could explore it, and our four-wheeling canyon adventure was refunded.

Pat and I ventured to a Phoenix grocery store and met barren shelves. The selection was limited, so we bought what we could and swallowed our anxiety. We hid the gloomy reality from the girls. They were sunk in a funk as the public pool at our last vacation spot closed. Our family felt trapped in the condo for the remaining two nights, and it was impossible to keep off of technology with the constant COVID updates.

Those nights in the Phoenix condo marked one of my more difficult parenting chapters. We all ran with higher-than-normal emotions and fears, and it was difficult to answer their many questions. I didn't have assurances to offer them; I was just as confused and scared. Our conversations looped as they pressed for details about our return home. National guidelines suggested quarantining 14 days after potential exposure, especially after travel. I looked at these two young ladies and tried to explain why they wouldn't return to their boyfriends or ordinary lives.

The cramped condo quarters only multiplied the tension surrounding our world's reality. Emotions across the board were high as we prepared to fly home with masks. I stared into the eyes of anyone (above that mask) within proximity. I looked at them as a human germ and dared them to infect my family.

Independent Warrior Daughter had no problem declaring her intentions once we got back to Duluth.

"I am going to see my boyfriend. I am an adult. You can ground me when I get back," she said.

Oh, sweet child, this is much bigger than your ego. Can you trust me even though I don't understand this more than you do?

I tried to reason, "He lives with his elderly grandmother, Michelle. How would you feel if you brought COVID into their household?"

The gravity of the situation fell flat on her immature ears, and we both refused to give in. She did the unexpected; she left. I couldn't tie her down and wouldn't stand in her way. Her newly budding love was essential, and she preferred to run off into the woods with him. My heart broke as I acknowledged my lack of control, but also her sheer willpower that chose to ignore me. While the world fell apart and we clung to those we loved the most, I had to say goodbye to my daughter. I intuitively understood our relationship as mother and daughter had just started a new chapter for us. Her timing felt all wrong, but when does your eldest leaving the nest feel right?

Pat's birthday was the Monday after we returned from vacation. At the end of the previous fall, he had reported a few unusual medical symptoms to his primary doctor, which had led him down a fairly extensive path of investigation to determine the cause. Unfortunately, he had a follow-up appointment on his birthday that didn't provide the best diagnosis. The newest lab results revealed a rare autoimmune disease that would alter his life indefinitely. COVID instantly became a fiercer threat to him, and his doctor's team worked to improve his immunity.

In this average week in March, COVID had chased us home from vacation, closed my school, and chased off my eldest daughter. Now my partner had a challenging medical journey ahead of him. To say I was overwhelmed is an understatement.

..

I was a COVID teacher. At the same time that society grasped at straws to find a sense of balance, my role as an educator held a whole new meaning. When the states shut down their educational systems in March 2020, it was safe to say the panic monster drove the educational bus. There wasn't a lot of rhyme or reason, and our district (and most of the world) hadn't prepared to teach virtually. So for my GEDO program, I scheduled weekly Google Hangout meetings with each student. I would appear on a screen to support and check in on each of them; I tried to be transparent and honest but also hide my high levels of discomfort.

"How are you? How is your mental health? Have you been able to work on anything for school? Can we set a goal for next week? I would prefer you wear a shirt while we meet," I said.

When virtual learning stripped the structure of the school building away, I relied on the strength of our previously built relationships to keep moving us toward graduation.

Virtual teaching was hard. Not seeing Michelle was harder. Sharing Camille with her other household during the pandemic was stressful. Watching Leila's mental health plummet was devastating. Understanding and rallying behind Pat's diagnosis were practically impossible. The needs of those around me consumed me, and self-care was not in my vocabulary. I was too busy trying to keep all the ducks in a row.

..

On May 25, 2020, the murder of George Floyd happened two hours south in Pat's previous neighborhood. His death at the knee of a Minneapolis police officer fueled conversations about racial injustices as citizens demanded to know how the United States intended to combat police misconduct and brutality and this systemic racism. The riots and fallout started close to home but quickly spread. The world showed up to support African Americans and demanded change. The nation looked to President Trump for guidance and comfort during this tragedy and the ongoing Covid-19 pandemic, but what he offered wasn't quieting the masses. It seemed we were imploding as a nation.

Pat and I needed to pick up furniture on the block of Floyd's murder only a month after the tragedy. Not only was the street filled with people, healing tents, and articles of the memorial, the atmosphere was what impacted me the most. There was an energy on that block that hung heavy, yet electrified. I could feel the tension, the sadness, and the anger as if the city blocks held those emotions tight in a bubble. The damage from the riots hadn't been cleaned up, and we had to crawl over debris to get into the shop's back entrance. After a month of being closed down, we were the first customers to visit her shop since Floyd's death. I cannot lie; the situation felt volatile and scary for a girl who had grown up in a town with three stop lights. My heart hurt, but I honestly didn't know how to participate in the movement for change.

..

Closing out the 2020 school year was emotional. Even though Michelle didn't move back to my home, we still had an important chapter coming to an end. Daughter #1 didn't have a graduation ceremony, and the class and community watched a taped slideshow from separate homes. She had no culminating SpringTrap experience. I hosted no grad party to honor her years of accomplishment. It just seemed so unfair. I watched a daughter and my students mourn the celebration they deserved but couldn't have. It was a harsh life lesson for them to face with little consolation.

After almost three months of virtual teaching, the countdown to summer break never sounded so good. The short reprieve would be enough to start the following fall with renewed energy, depending on what happened with our pandemic. It would HAVE TO be over by the fall.

Pat had lived with me for about a month when we decided to put my Superior home on the market and move back across the bridge to Duluth. He seemed committed to our future, even though there was still much distress with his children back in the Cities. My 1892 home was unique and beautiful but also ancient. I could not afford the updates it already needed. With Pat's financial partnership, we could afford an updated home in which we could all be comfortable. We found a mid-century modern ranch-style home that we loved and bid aggressively. My own home sold the same day it went on the market. Both deals were in place, and we were set to relocate.

Packing a home during COVID was a great distraction. Time wasn't in short supply, and most of our belongings got stored in the garage, ready for transfer. A significant purge moved unnecessary items to the curb to become someone else's treasure. That June, after we moved, the energy at the new home was lighter and brighter and an overall improvement. I loved this home and the outlook for the future. I could never have predicted how short of a time I would spend at this address on Sussex Avenue.

..

In the heart of COVID, four years after the last exchange with my friend, Liz, I still hadn't stopped thinking about her. I watched some of her life changes on Facebook, but no more than that. Recently her posts had changed, and I intuitively felt I should reach out to her. I was thrilled that she responded, and we shared the blessings and curses we had both gone through within our family dynamics and COVID. We were both guarded but willing to meet for coffee at some point.

Months later, I walked to a city lake park in Liz's hometown. I glanced at the lovely woman who sat on a park bench and waited with coffee. She looked the same, yet different all at once. Her posture was more poised, yet the girl I came to love as a 17-year-old was there too.

We hugged, and I held her tightly. Tears streamed unchecked down my cheeks as we whispered apologies and words of love into the ear of the other. We sat on the park bench in the sun and shared. It felt like coming home. Our visit wasn't long enough, but our connection fused back together. We were two sovereign and bonded women.

We brought our families together when she came to stay for a weekend in Duluth. Michelle and Leila went into her arms as I watched and shed emotional tears. Their relationship had been so meaningful as young children, yet it had been severed entirely over the recent years. Time turned back a decade as the girls lounged in the hammock outside while Liz read them a children's book from a nearby chair. That long weekend together healed our hearts.

Soon after, I drove my daughters toward the Cities to see her family for the day. We dined, played, and bonded. A photograph captured the seven smiling female faces as we lived our best life together. I thought we had created a new tribe.

..

Those summer months offered me a great window of time to regroup and ground. After months of extensive hiking, I felt physically and mentally ready for the start of the new school year. Before the end of summer, my school district rolled out solid plans for the upcoming year. Our school district decided a hybrid model to be the safest path with so many COVID unknowns. Students were offered either hybrid or entirely virtual learning for the upcoming school year. Students that chose hybrid attended classes in the building two days a week—my reduced GEDO classes allowed for extensive, quality check-ins and relationship building. Student attendance and success held at high levels, and I was grateful the students embraced this unique experience. This was the most reasonable work schedule I had ever had. I cherished the Wednesdays for teachers to regroup, refresh, and hold meetings from home.

As the first months of the school year ticked by, we moved into cooler temps and a new season of COVID and Pat's disease. Our teaching reverted to entirely virtual to keep infection numbers in check. By mid-November, I sat at the formal dining room table in the center of my home and wondered where my summer balance had disappeared. The world, my life, and this household were spinning haphazardly. I managed my virtual teaching schedule to support students. Leila gave up her title as senior volleyball captain to transition into college classes. Our two puppies ran the house quite literally and demanded attention. My body was overwhelmed with this new amount of pet dander and itched and twitched regularly. Camille enrolled in 1st grade, and her new school's virtual schedule was rigorous, with four daily Zoom classes and computer assignments. She despised school as she knew it, and I watched her mental health deteriorate.

No matter how many holes I plugged in the boat, it still was taking on water. Pat's physical and mental health crumbled, and he walked around the house with a heavy cloak of despair. My mask of sanity was held in place by the barest of threads. When I needed an escape, it seemed the only place I could hide was in the shower. Sometimes I tried to wash away the weight on my chest two or three times a day and hoped those anxiety germs would wash down the drain.

Our partnership had been going downhill for months. I had overlooked a lot of it because I just didn't have room to process it. Then, finally, I came out of the fog of his disease, the move across the bridge, and the education change for every family member. I woke up and saw some gaping truths staring at me, making me very uncomfortable. My therapist, Missy, was the first person to challenge me.

"Why do you feel you must stay with Pat?" she asked.

Her question caught me off guard, mainly because it scared me but also because I trusted her judgment.

I vocalized all the reasons I needed to stay unhappy, "Well, he isn't healthy, and I sold my house, and I have this new house, and my girls can't keep moving, and it's COVID."

I strung that all out in one sentence without a breath.

As soon as I gave her question space, I became honest with myself. This carnival ride had so many layers! I admitted I wasn't happy with my partner. I felt disrespected. I walked on eggshells. After my previous experiences, I knew I needed to share my feelings with him and hoped for a willingness to work on our relationship.

Those conversations didn't go well. Pat and I got into heated arguments, and neither of us refused to back down. He wouldn't accept much accountability, and we arrived at an impasse. I needed to feel differently, and he needed me not to.

The relationship dissolved on Thanksgiving of 2020, but COVID made it challenging to make arrangements to separate. As a result, we decided to wait another six months to go our separate ways.

I smacked my forehead in disbelief, "What the fuck have I done?"
..

Both big girls and their boyfriends got COVID the week of Christmas. While the big girls weren't at our home much, Leila had been there for two hours while contagious. Her positive results sent me to one of our testing sites to find out if I was also infected. I canceled Christmas plans, and Camille stayed with her dad until my results returned. I spent the holiday watching movies and eating Campbell's soup. Thankfully, my results returned negative the day after Christmas, and I got Camille to our home to celebrate.

Our home was unusually tense while Pat lived in the basement. Late-night texts came from the basement on Christmas Eve. His messages held swords of rage and accusation.

"You didn't mask up before you got your results back. How dare you try to kill me!" Pat said.

Before my results arrived, I had stayed on the main level while he had been on the lower level. I honestly hadn't considered using one, nor had he asked me to put one on the couple of times he walked through. His accusations were intense and scared me, yet he refused to respond to any of my texts. His communication was one-way only.

There wasn't a lot I could do. I couldn't turn back time and put a mask on my face for those few days.

"If he won't even have a conversation with me, why should I apologize?" My stubbornness stood firm and only intensified when his one-way threats continued. I realized our shared household might not hold out for multiple months, but I didn't have the energy to think about it.

Before May 2021

"I understand now that I'm not a mess but a deeply feeling
person in a messy world. I explain that now, when someone asks me why I cry so often, I say, 'For the same reason
I laugh so often - because I'm paying attention.'"

– Glennon Doyle Melton, *The Minds Journal*

On Thursday, January 8th, 2021, Leila returned from a date and placed her leftovers in the fridge. In a simple-enough scenario, Pat ate them without asking permission, and my middle daughter saw red. Leila felt a lot of stress over the situation that unfolded in our home, and his eating her food was the straw that broke the camel's back. She started a texting exchange to confront him, which quickly escalated to a face-to-face confrontation. The topic of argument quickly changed from leftovers to my attempted murder of him. Leila tried to defend me but was a weak match to an intoxicated adult. His cold fingers tried to clamp over her neck as he lunged at her. Luckily, she escaped from his room and ran directly to mine.

We left. Leila went to her boyfriend's house. Arlo, the puppy, went to Michelle's house. I traveled to Two Harbors to sleep on my best friend's couch. My momma bear instincts didn't like going separate ways at such a tumultuous time, but we had limited options. So, in turmoil, I contacted our women's shelter for advice.

"Are your family members safe? I am sorry you had to go through that. Here is the contact person to reach out to tomorrow for more information," they explained.

Fear and anger kept me up the entire night before I brushed my teeth and headed to work. I had so many pieces to figure out, but going to work was predictable, and I needed autopilot. Soon after I arrived at work, he texted me.

"I changed the locks. As a result, you are not allowed back into the house. I am considering contacting my lawyer to draw up murder charges against you," he wrote.

I was 45 years old, homeless with two children and a puppy during the January of COVID. I had nothing but the clothes on my body. I sat in my desk chair and simply stared out my classroom window at the dingy white snowbanks outside. I briefly wondered if I could stay in my classroom for the night, but that wasn't a solution. I took a deep breath and humbly explained my situation to Jodelle and Joey so that they could keep and support Camille over the next few days. Next, I had to find a couch for the night and figure out how to get some of our belongings. These two steps seemed monumental, and I couldn't see anything past them.

Our names were both on the title of the Sussex house, and the cops escorted me to the door to gather essentials. Pat greeted the officers and me, shaking a paper in his hand, saying I couldn't enter until I signed it.

"I am not signing anything right now. I just want to gather some belongings for the girls and me," I said.

He nodded his head manically, and there was no question he was unbalanced. Yes, I had the RIGHT to be back in my house, but he also had the RIGHT to be there. His bark was bigger than mine, and I was scared of him. For the next 20 minutes, I made a mad dash to grab and stash the essential items to take with me. This house I had grown to love already felt dark and intimidating in the 48 hours since I had been there. The heaviness bore down on me, and I wasted no time before leaving.

He hadn't backed down from his string of hate emails and texts. Pat threatened multiple times to show up at my school and talk to my principal.

Part of me laughed at this, "What? Do you think my principal will give me detention? Fire me?"

The other part of me was concerned he would be crazy enough to show up and cause drama. I swallowed my pride again and showed my school liaison and administration the emails so that people were on alert. As his threats to press murder charges against me continued, I was terrified. I knew I hadn't tried to kill him, but I also didn't have a lot of faith in our justice system. Pat's longtime lawyer happened to be the representative for Derek Chauvin, the Minneapolis officer on trial for the murder of George Floyd. This lawyer had clout, and I wasn't sure if he would be willing to hear Pat's attempted murder claim.

I saw the emotional effects of my plunders wash across the faces of my children yet again. Pat held the rest of our household possessions (which was mostly everything) for ransom until I met his demands. There was no magic wand for me to wave to improve this situation with urgency. Still looking for secure housing, I had much less time with Camille. My mental health wasn't in the best space to be a good mom right now, but being separated from her was costing both of us. She was my light and joy. I felt bad enough that her home was gone, but I didn't consider the ramifications of dropping off a letter at Pat's house with her in the car. Camille's English Cream Retriever sensed her presence as I pulled up to drop off that letter and jumped to the window seat to peer out. I turned around in the car front seat and saw utter turmoil in my youngest daughter's eyes as she looked at her puppy. My tears fell; I sucked as a mother.

I worked hard to find the best temporary situation for me and the girls. I found safe spaces for a couple of weeks at friends' homes and a few months at a furnished rental. After I had signed agreements with Pat, some fantastic women helped me pack a 2600-square-foot house in less than six hours. We threw much of the belongings in the garbage because that's what time would allow, and at this point, much of the household items just felt like extra baggage. I was back at rock bottom, but even this little progress went a long way.

..

The day Pat changed the locks and I found myself officially home-less, I reached out to one of my support sisters, Liz. His onslaught of nasty text messages had me unraveling, and I needed compassionate help. Elizabeth offered me her ear and first-hand experience with her recent partner. She could relate to the panic I tried to rein in; she also understood the devastation and innate need to protect our babies.

I didn't hear from her for the next few days of phone calls, planning, and couch jumping. It took me a whole month before I got my feet on the ground and could formulate a rational thought. Even though I had found a safe, furnished apartment for three months, that didn't quiet the drama and trauma that came from the sidelines. My attempts to untangle myself from Pat were all I had the energy to focus on outside of my children, teaching, and the ongoing pandemic.

One month turned into two without a word from Liz. Three months after the implosion of my world, I celebrated my 46th birthday. It went unrecognized by her, and I needed to understand her silence.

I sent a one-word message the day after my birthday, "Hello?"

Liz called soon after I sent the text, but my heart lodged in my throat, and I couldn't answer. Finally, she left a message and apologized for not contacting me on my birthday. The remainder of her message included standard "busy with life" excuses.

My birthday wasn't why I had reached out as I had.

What I asked was, "Hi. Are you okay? I hurt that you haven't checked in on me for the past few months. I am doing better, but I have a long way to go. I sure could use a visit or a hug."

I replied to her voice message via text, "Thanks for the call. I was just checking in on you. Hope all is well, and the Spring makes everyone feel good."

I took a long, hard look at what I wanted this friendship to be and compared it to what it was. Finally, I permitted myself to let Liz go.

..

A 2021 GEDO student inspired me to wipe the dust off my tarot and oracle decks to share space with her. This young lady wanted to understand something much bigger than life, which reminded me of my quest for something "better." My oracle and tarot deck came out after the other students left, and Jess stayed to talk spiritual woo-woo stuff. She was a catalyst for my dive back into the world of intuition and cards, only this time, I didn't bring any reservations.

I needed someone or something to guide my life because I gave up. I threw my hands in the air and shouted, "I quit!" I hoped there would be guidance in the messages of my card readings from someone or something wiser than me. Reading oracle and tarot spreads became a part of my everyday practice. Sometimes I would search for specific answers, and other times I would just allow messages to come through. As I got more convinced of the validity of the communications from unpredictable synchronicities and occurrences, I watched YouTube videos of "professional" readers. The cards acknowledged my deep pain, often pointing back to a mother wound. Many times the messages encouraged me to have more faith in myself and to believe in my ability to be healthy and successful. How does someone give up control and be in flow? I learned to trust my inner voice and feel sensations in my body that had always guided and directed me; I had just never chosen to listen. A new communication channel opened up, and I was ready to listen.

I started recognizing specific angel numbers that popped up, and I got curious about their meaning. The two numbers that I regularly saw at this time were 911 and 922. According to Google, "The angel number 911 suggests that you are on the right path and should trust your intuition. You are on the road to finding your true purpose in life and the right people to surround yourself with." With the number 922, I had seen this number for several years and felt pretty annoyed with the Universe. That angel number is Mother's birthday, and I didn't appreciate having it thrown in my face regularly. I thought maybe I was supposed to turn the other cheek (for the 21st time) and try to repair our broken relationship. However, it wasn't until I looked up the spiritual meaning of 922 that I understood the message. Angel numbers can have myriad implications, but the definition I found when I searched was this: Have belief in yourself. You are strong enough and intelligent enough to create the life you desire.

Feeling worthy and like I was enough was one of my biggest battles due to the consequences of my childhood. This angel message wanted me to know that I am so much more than what Mother encouraged me to be.

..

Over the past months I had relied on my sister, Ann, more than ever before. She stepped up and started thinking through the tasks and systems I needed back in place, which was invaluable support. During those first weeks, she was my "taskmaster," and I even forwarded my mail to her address. We talked and saw each other often, which is probably why the phone call I received from Leila devastated me.

This weekend morning, I stood in the tiny kitchen of my furnished dwelling and took a call from Daughter #2.

"Have you heard about Ann?"

My sister and family recently left for a trip to Florida and Disney, and my heart sank and jumped to the conclusion that something had happened.

Leila said, "She's pregnant."

A flood of emotions washed over me: delight, joy, confusion, and disbelief. My sister hadn't mentioned anything about trying for a third baby, and the news came as a shock. As I processed Leila's two-word statement, the confusion sank in. How did she know and I didn't?

"What do you mean? How do you know?" I asked.

"Dad told me. Grandpa told him a couple of days ago," she answered.

With that understanding, my heart cracked open, and words were, again, frozen in my throat. My abusive ex-husband had known about my only sister's pregnancy before I did. The pecking order of the family was once again at play. Betrayal slammed into my chest, and I couldn't end this phone call with my daughter fast enough.

"I need to go. I can't talk about this right now," I cried.

I heard my voice laced with panic, but I didn't care. The news of Ann's pregnancy rocked my world more than it should, but how? Why? I had just seen her a couple of days earlier. When I was alone with my thoughts minutes later, I sank to my knees and cried.

Missy helped me work through a new layer of pain as I formulated the most honest, vulnerable letter for my sister I had ever written. I hand-wrote about the years of struggle with mom and dad allowing Leif in their life. Their choices made me feel like the pain and abuse I endured were acceptable behavior. Then, I dove into my pent-up feelings about Ann being in the messy middle and how that made me feel unsupported. To end my letter, I shared this new, deep pain that she hadn't shared the good news directly with me, and I had learned it down the pipeline.

She answered my letter. Ann texted me her own feelings and distress over being in the middle of our family. Our dad shouldn't have told Leif, and she apologized that I had heard that way.

"You don't know how hard it has been with Mom and Dad pressuring me why I still have you in my life. I told them we are sisters, and our bond hadn't changed."

My abandoned inner child focused on the fact that my parents were still disgusted by me and didn't even want me to have a relationship with my sister. If it was possible, my heart broke a little more; it was the first confirmation that my parents weren't working toward drawing me back into their life. They were actively trying to REMOVE people.

I had been trying to find housing for my daughters and me only two months prior. This new assault tipped the scales, and I could no longer hide the fact that I needed to be supported 100% for my trauma and abuse, or not at all. My sister hanging in the messy middle had gone on for almost nine years, and I couldn't accept that for myself anymore. I also realized that Ann was in the same delusional trance I had been in, and she couldn't possibly validate what I had gone through.

I walked away from my sister, brother-in-law, and two dear nephews because I didn't have any other choice if I wanted to honor myself.

..

Even though I had stable housing, the emotions I tried to process around Pat, my sister, and my friend Liz were fairly monumental and more than I could handle alone. Missy, my therapist, had been my rock and support for over six years, and I turned to her again. Session by session, she helped me unpack my feelings to understand my identity and priorities better. In one particular session, she held up a book titled *Homecoming* by John Bradshaw.

"This book better explains our inner child and potential blockages. I think you might like how it digs into family aspects," she said.

Even though my more recent trauma was related to a partner, I figured I'd read it. I didn't grab it with vigor; I just ordered it on Amazon as an afterthought from her recommendation. Reading that book was the single most impactful part of my healing journey. Its back cover captured my attention when it suggested I was making crappy adult decisions due to my childhood trauma. Say what?!

I gave my inner child the space she deserved for the first time ever. I started exploring the book with an open mind, but I wasn't prepared for the tsunami of emotions that swamped me. In *Homecoming's* prologue, the author shares a story of a man walking around an Inner Child Support Group as he listens to the stories told by its members. An older gray-haired man is reading a letter his inner child had written to his father; my heart lurches and connects instantly, and I grab tissues before I even turn to page two. Chapter One starts by telling me my inner child is contaminating and sabotaging my life. And here I thought it was an ancient voodoo hex!

Many of the symptoms of a wounded inner child resonated with me, like co-dependence, trust issues, emptiness, intimacy dysfunctions, and magical beliefs. So I grabbed a nearby pen and started underlining the concepts that struck a chord, and it wasn't long before I saw how much I needed to reclaim my wounded inner child. Bradshaw prepared me for the dramatic journey of returning to my broken childhood places to patch, repair, and nourish what needed fixing. My ego figured this would be easy!

The book would guide me through five different phases of childhood: infancy, toddler, preschool age, school age, and adolescence. Most of the difficulties I faced with my parents happened during adolescence and young adulthood, and I prepared for the book's results to match my experiences. As I took the quiz assigned to the infancy phase, the first nine months of life, my affirmative answers started adding up:

Do you find it hard to trust other people?

Do you ignore good nutrition or fail to get enough exercise?

Do you have deep fears of abandonment? Have you ever felt desperate because a love relationship ended?

The 16 questions varied greatly and even asked about intimacy preferences. At the end of the quiz, I tallied my 'yes' responses at 13/16. I figured these results were a fluke and flipped ahead to the Toddler Quiz in the next chapter, only NOT to have similar results. My inner child had been traumatized as an infant! I could see her need for love and belonging had made all the decisions in my life, and most didn't put me in a good place.

I learned so much just from taking the quizzes and was astounded, yet accepting, of the results. I reached down to my wounded inner child and walked her through the meditation and affirmation activities for each category. Tears stained the letters as my left hand wrote a scribbled inner child letter to adult Heather, crying out to be held and loved. I painstakingly wrote that little girl the most emotional love letter I had ever written, enveloping her in pure, selfless love and support. The imagery during the meditations united and bonded me with my previous childhood phases. In the last raw and emotional capstone meditation, each version of Heather walked up, hand in hand, to confront our parents. We voiced our pain and released their parenting responsibility from our lives before we turned our backs and walked away whole.

..

Nothing was more important to me than finding a new home to purchase and move into. The apartment lacked permanency, and that made me feel ungrounded. My inner child and I both craved a new home to start over in. Unfortunately, COVID still had an influence on the housing market, and it was insanely out of balance. Homes received multiple offers on the same day they listed, and there wasn't time to hesitate. I wanted an affordable sanctuary that met my family's needs as soon as possible, but my first two offers didn't work out. I had moved nine times in a decade and wanted this part DONE!

My puppy, Arlo, had escaped to a neighbor's yard the first few weeks while couch-jumping. I grabbed him from next door, but not before we got invited in for a quick visit. I explained that Arlo and I were staying next door for a short time as I looked for a home.

"We might know someone that is selling in Lakeside. She has a nice house only a few blocks away," the neighbor lady said.

Their friend had relocated to the Cities during COVID to help with grandchildren and hadn't lived in the home for a while. I wasn't told any details about the home: not the address, size, age, or even the price. It was a house that MIGHT be going on the market. I wasn't willing to be optimistic and was too tired to get my hopes up, but I gave her my number in case it became available. The next day I received a phone call to see that mysterious house down the road. I still wasn't getting my hopes up.

I pulled my car up to a small, well-taken-care-of bungalow on Otsego Street.

"Wow, isn't that cute! Okay, don't get too excited," I told myself.

When we walked into the front door and then the kitchen, I started to cry. I felt this home envelop me in the warmest hug and greet me with wide-open arms. I intuitively knew it was a sanctuary to place roots, find peace, and restart. Moments later, my panic monster showed up and delivered a hefty dose of anxiety and fear that something so beautiful would never work out for me. I stared that beast in the eye and said, "Back off."

..

Spring Break arrived two months after being displaced. I had packed up my previous home in a matter of hours and settled into a small, furnished apartment for the time being. COVID was still dictating education and our world. I was tired. I didn't have the money or energy to take off anywhere tropical like I had to Arizona a couple of years back, but I knew I deserved a get-away. I wanted peace and solace in some remote location without glitz or glamor or humans. After some AirBnb research, I found exactly what I longed for in the back of a horse pasture in Spooner, Wisconsin. An older couple had created a wall tent oasis on the back of their 40 acres, with a mission to offer tenants a secluded space without the noise of life. I packed up my car, grabbed the pup, and headed for our Spring Break retreat.

We arrived after dark and found our prepared tent in the woods, with a fire in the stove and twinkling lights and candles inviting us inside. Our adventure was modest with a water cooler, woodstove, and outdoor privy, but I sank onto the comfortable bed and let myself relax. Over the next few days, I hiked with Arlo in the snow, meditated, cried, and had a few spiritual epiphanies. Surprisingly, my diva Arlo was a natural farm dog. He made friends with the owner's doodles and horses; I think he appreciated the lighter atmosphere as much as I did. While he explored and scampered, I sat and enjoyed the company of Max and Rochelle, the owners. We sat contentedly on their deck, absorbing the new radiant sun of mid-March while sharing stories and smiles. Their gentle nature made me feel more content and happy than I had been in weeks. We continued our visits that weekend, and by the end, I had asked them to adopt me (my inner child knew that these were good people). While we never filed adoption paperwork, I accepted these two special humans into my tribe and considered them family.

..

In the end, the panic monster had it all wrong. The seller, offer, and timeline all fell into place for us to move into that adorable bungalow in Lakeside. I had new tears to shed, but these tears were laced with joy and gratitude. The girls and I happily transferred into that special sanctuary at the end of April with the promise of spring and rebirth around us. There was another home to unpack, but this time it felt different. I took my time and wasn't in a hurry, letting the sanctuary guide me. I languished in these walls' safety and comfort and believed she had called us to her. We named her "Victoria, Goddess of Victory."

I made promises to myself when I moved into that new home. I committed to living life MY WAY, without worrying about acceptance or permission from anyone. I promised to focus on the beauty I could create for myself and my daughters. I declared it a time for smiles, laughter, and unconditional love for everyone. It was time to start a new chapter.

Epilogue

"Of all the people you will know in a lifetime, you are the only one you will never leave nor lose. To the question of your life, you are the only answer. To the problems of your life, you are the only solution."

— Jo Coudert, *Advice from a Failure*

Of course, the story doesn't end there. That was just another starting point in my life when I took up residency in my Lakeside 1950s bungalow. I am happy to announce that Victoria (my Goddess home) and my two-year anniversary will be in a few months, and I have said many times that I will never sell her.

Today, as I sit in my office chair and type out the last lines of my year-long book project, I genuinely love myself. What an epic feeling! I have cried as many tears through the joys of my growth as the sorrows of my struggles. My journey to self-love began with some pretty painful experiences. I became an adult very comfortable with being a codependent martyr, willing to point and blame. It's easy to feel sad, mad, or offended by the actions of others, but in the end, I was the common denominator. When I first considered writing a memoir, my lens was about capturing the absurd details of my life and sensationalizing them, "Hasn't my life been crap!?" It's no wonder the Universe froze up my creative juices until I better understood WHY I should share my story.

Changing directions and starting over multiple times in mid-life wasn't easy. I certainly faked it a lot. I feigned strength and confidence when inside I felt alone and petrified. I had many ah-ha moments and a few long, hard looks in the mirror to wake me up and realize creating a better life was up to me and nobody else. My tiny changes often created the momentum of a giant snowball rolling down a hill, gaining magnitude and momentum and surprised me when I was able to look in the rearview mirror. For the record, this written account is about ME. The others in the book played an invaluable role in my awakening, but I worked hard to find the grace to write this book with integrity instead of ill will. I have released myself from their control and continue to heal.

I also didn't intend to get so good at telling people goodbye, although the facts suggest otherwise. I have always craved pure, authentic love, and I don't consider myself cold or closed-off. On the contrary, as my self-love started forming, I faced many difficult choices about the energy and people I allowed. I have gotten to the point that if you aren't "for me" and my continued growth, I must do a hard pass. The beauty is that as I removed people, I couldn't yet see that I was making space for new people and experiences that would give me new love and life.

It isn't chance that I became a successful teacher of students who had experienced trauma. I learned to be a good listener and to resist judgment completely. I subscribe to the great value of solid, clear communication and the power of actual vulnerability. That's what I brought into my classroom. I didn't become an intuitive empath because I uncovered any unique spiritual gifts. I became a sensitive seer because I previously needed to predict and feel the room's energy to survive. I learned to notice the subtle changes in facial expressions, tone of voice, or body language because it is what I did to stay "safe." I don't walk into a room searching for the happiest person; my eyes rove for anyone with weird vibes. I still do that. You won't be able to fool me with your words or appearance; I can see you. Sometimes that scares people, making them feel vulnerable and exposed. All I can do is shrug my shoulders and say, "Sorry."

I chose to write this book as a celebration - for me, for my girls, and for any other human who feels life has given them a tough hand. You are never alone. It's difficult to admit, but I wasn't special because of my life experiences, and neither are you. I know that sounds crass, but it's the truth. Nobody cares about your life more than you do, which means the only way to change your circumstances is to stand on your own two feet and do something about it. So what's the tiniest change you can make right now that positively impacts your life? That's where it starts. That's where faking something better turns into ripples that can turn into waves; then, we work toward the magic. Every damn one of us is worth living a magically decorated life. I invite you to join me.

"For you, a thousand times over."
– Khaled Hosseini, *The Kite Runner*

Acknowledgments

Missy Nervick - You were my guidance and clarity. Thank you for seeing and believing in me when I couldn't offer that to myself. My healing and accomplishments couldn't have happened without you, my friend.

Sarah Seidelmann, Inger Kenobi & my *Let's Fly Friends* - Your invitation and space to write changed my life. Sarah, thank you for the guided meditations that allowed me to see this book as its own energy and to understand my role was simply to support it. Inger, you drilled into my head these priceless considerations, "Where's the joy leading you?" and "What's the easy button?" And to the Flapping Group, thanks for being a unique community where I continue to feel fully, vulnerably myself. A new tribe.

Cyndee Parsons - I smile at our years of friendship that conveniently moved you into my basement when I needed you (and your wine) most through the last phases of this book. Your insight and suggestions helped soften my rough edges and kept my toes pointed forward.

Vincent Herrera, *Tami Morrison*, and *Francy Chammings* - my beta readers and editor, you read through some intensely weak rough draft baloney. Your efforts, feedback, and suggestions were invaluable. Thank you for your vital role in keeping my boat afloat!

Florentine Maréchal @ Nooordic Creative Studio - When looking for an intuitive soulpreneur to help design "Me," I couldn't predict finding a soul-sister across the ocean. Thank you for the branding, website, and book design - your masterpieces brought me to tears on many occasions. Cheers to the "April 7th Aries Flo & Heather Show!"

My *Daughters* - We live up to the definition of unconditional love and support - we are family. Thank you for switching hats to support me, your momma, and understanding that this story needed to be shared.

My *Floodwood, ALC & GEDO* students - I consider all of you lifetime members of my dysfunctional family. Our relationship might have been teacher and student, but always remember how much you offered me. In many ways, you saved me.

I cannot leave without offering homage to the authors that left an imprint on my heart and soul, guiding and inspiring me to write my own story.

Cheryl Strayed, *Wild*

Jeannette Walls, *The Glass Castle*

Khaled Hosseini, *The Kite Runner*

Elizabeth Gilbert, *Big Magic*

Brené Brown, *Braving the Wilderness*

Gabrielle Bernstein, *The Universe Has Your Back*

Pat Solomon, *Finding Joe Documentary. Joseph Campbell's hero journey*

Connect with the Author

HezzieMae.com

Facebook.com/HeatherN.Wilde

LinkeIn/HeathrN.Wilde

Leave a Review

If you enjoyed reading *Tumbled*, please consider leaving a review with your book distributor or the platform of your choice. Reviews help self-published authors find more readers just like you.

About The Author

Heather N. Wilde is an indie publisher, writer, speaker, artist, and trauma survivor. She is the author of *Tumbled: A Memoir or Perseverance, Personal Growth & Magical Transformation*, *Pig Tales and Popcorn: Patricia's Memoir*, and *Sell Your Book, Not Your Soul*. She watercolor-illustrated *Precious Child*, a timeless children's book. In 2023, Heather founded Hezzie Mae, an indie publishing company. She speaks on accountability, personal growth, and recovering from trauma with the potential to lead an extraordinary life.